With humor and heartfelt insights, God Is in This Fight will strengthen your faith and provide clarity during your waiting moments – this is a must-read for anyone ready to pursue God's calling.

Laurie Swink
Co-founder of Selah Freedom

Having known Ted and the journey behind Invisible Angels since its early stages, it's both moving and inspiring to see firsthand how unwavering faith and obedience to God's calling have paved a way for survivors of human trafficking to find real freedom. This book is far more than a testimony – it's a source of hope and a reminder that persistence in the face of adversity can lead to amazing breakthroughs. Ted's story will inspire readers to stay the course, especially when pursuing their God-given purpose feels overwhelming.

Glory Coronati
Executive Director, Free Indeed

GOD
IS IN THIS
FIGHT

GOD
IS IN THIS
FIGHT

HOW GOD MADE A WAY TO RESCUE
HUMAN TRAFFICKING SURVIVORS

TED GREENFIELD

ANEKO
PRESS

Aneko Press

www.anekopress.com

Aneko Press, Life Sentence Publishing, and our logos are trademarks of

Life Sentence Publishing, Inc.
203 E. Birch Street
P.O. Box 652
Abbotsford, WI 54405

BIOGRAPHY & AUTOBIOGRAPHY / Religious

Paperback ISBN: 979-8-88936-503-7

Book ISBN: 979-8-88936-504-4

10 9 8 7 6 5 4 3 2 1

Available where books are sold

CONTENTS

INTRODUCTION

Human trafficking, in various forms, has existed for millennia. In Acts 16:16-19, a young slave girl can predict the future. Suddenly, her owners are left profitless when she spiritually identifies Paul and his traveling companions as *"servants of the Most High God, who are telling you the way to be saved."* In chapter 5 of 2 Kings, it is outright admitted that a young girl was taken captive to serve Naaman's wife, and in Genesis 30, there is the trading of young women for the sole purpose of sexual pleasure and producing offspring.

Today, human trafficking is a caustically corrosive reality that is just beginning to gain the attention and awareness it desperately needs. However, due to the depravity of our condition, its presence in our modern-day society is nothing new. From Genesis to today, there has been, and is currently, the selling of people, young and old, men and women, and boys and girls for sex and slave labor. Sadly, nothing has changed since the fall. The question both believers and unbelievers have is, Why? Why would a loving God allow this to happen?

The simple answer is: Satan was given a significant foothold in this world, as we see in Genesis 3.

Today, six thousand years or so from Genesis 3, the human

condition hasn't changed at all. In the United States and throughout the rest of the world, people are still being bought, sold, and held captive for sex and slave labor. Peeling back the layers and taking a deeper look, today's reality is just as grotesque. Most trafficking survivors are lured in by someone they know, usually a family member. The very people who are there to protect God's children are selling them.

In my brief time since starting Invisible Angels we have provided emergency air transportation to rescue survivors, ranging from a child under the age of ten, whose parent sold him for child pornography, to an eighteen-year-old girl in the foster-care system who was sold for sex by her foster-care case worker, to a woman in her late forties who simply wound up in an extremely bad situation. Human trafficking is a violently uncomfortable topic, and human trafficking awareness needs to be raised by magnitudes beyond current levels.

In 2023, in the United States, the National Human Trafficking Hotline received over 30,000 signals (contacts), with over 7,000 coming from survivors of human trafficking. Through these contacts, the hotline identified over 9,000 cases involving over 16,000 victims.[1] These are just the reported cases. Statistics are very hard to measure accurately due to the fact that most human trafficking crimes go unreported.

The reality is that human trafficking is happening in every major city in America. The actual numbers may be much higher. Traffickers make between $150,000 and $200,000 annually per victim, often selling a young boy or girl for sex up to twelve times a day. Human trafficking has been replacing drug trafficking due to one simple fact: you can only sell a drug once, but you can sell a person over and over again.

In some places and cases, law enforcement may not be properly resourced. With the topic alone struggling to gain awareness,

---

1   Human Trafficking Statistics in the United States, *www.tbmlawyers.com/blog/ us-human-trafficking-statistics*.

combined with an overwhelmed legal system, justice may be extremely difficult because trafficking cases have to be proven in a courtroom. Just imagine what is facing a scared and confused young adult with no family and no resources when asked to testify against a trafficker, while simultaneously looking at the unspeakable reality of what traffickers will do to victims when they are crossed.

Although what we do may seem dangerous, it is not. This is not the movies. While there is risk, we do have security protocols and precautions in place. Local, state, and federal law enforcement are only eager to help.

Invisible Angels provides free, convenient, on-demand air transport, getting survivors where they need to be quickly, quietly, and almost invisibly. Our prayer for every flight is: "Lord, let the most exciting thing that happens be what we see out the window." That prayer has been answered on every flight so far.

The trafficking cases Invisible Angels addresses are all identified and referred by our dedicated partners in human trafficking rescue organizations and law enforcement. They are the real heroes on the front lines. We are privileged to work alongside individuals and organizations led by a staff of on-fire, born-again believers who share an amazing testimony of how God has led them into this fight and supplied them with everything they needed along the way. I am consistently amazed beyond belief, in every aspect of Ephesians 3:20, by the testimonies of the people leading these organizations in this fight, and by constantly seeing God perform lifesaving miracles over and over again.

While the circumstances behind each flight become increasingly challenging, I'm not deterred or discouraged. Instead, it deepens my sense of awe. God has given me a front seat and a role to play in the repeated miracles unfolding. The mere fact that God equips those He calls, rather than calling those already equipped, has been my life since 2018. I never expected to be involved in this way. I simply raised my hand one day, saying, "I want to get involved, so you can send me." I had no earthly idea it would evolve into this.

The miracles you are about to discover in the Invisible Angels' story didn't happen alone; they happened through devoted people who saw what God was doing with a complete stranger and jumped in to help.

I'm deeply grateful to rescue organizations like Selah Freedom, whose co-founder, Laurie Swink, has been a constant source of friendship and encouragement. The shared journey of non-profit start-up struggles, with both tears and joy, has been made lighter by Glori Coronati from Free Indeed, Brandy Crisafulli from Life Recaptured, Jamie and Tami Kent from No More, and Liz Perrault from Wings of the Way. Your collective love, support, and encouragement have been remarkable.

I'm deeply grateful for the many friends, both new and old, that God brought into my life during this time. Your belief and financial support were crucial. Thank you to Aimee, Angie, Ann, Big B, Bill Strong, Brian Cheetham, Craig and Ann Annonsen, Danielle, Danny, Dan and Carol Boone, Dave Bear, Dee, Dimitri, Ed, Hil, Jason, JoEllen, John, Judy, Karina, Karen, Kelly Carter, Kevin, Lisa, Lola, Lyla and Doug, Maria, Mark, Nancy and Caleb, Nico, Norm, Paul Bashould, Stephen and Joy, and the incredible support of City of God Church, Generation Church, Lake City Church, National Community Church, Radiant Church, and The Way of Messiah Fellowship. You are all the hands and feet of Jesus, and I couldn't have done this without you.

CHAPTER 1

THANK YOU FOR SAVING MY LIFE

Rescue me, Lord, from evildoers; protect me
from the violent, who devise evil plans in their
hearts and stir up war every day. They make
their tongues as sharp as a serpent's; the poison
of vipers is on their lips. (Psalm 140:1-3 NIV)

Nineteen minutes after takeoff, we touched down again, just long enough to save a life. We picked up our survivor and her advocate at a private terminal, then lifted off as quickly as we'd landed. Our destination: a safe house over a thousand miles to the north. This marked the third rescue for Invisible Angels, and God's miracles were happening so quickly that I could hardly keep up with them. Eight months earlier, Invisible Angels had been nothing more than a thought, a single God-given inspiration downloaded straight into my heart. We had no website, cards, or bank account. Just a vision. I had ideas upon ideas on where to take Invisible Angels, but God gave me the next steps to take as needed.

Now, as I hugged the coastline at fifty-five hundred feet, I realized we owned a $250,000 aircraft in perfect condition and that was mission-ready. Switching to the tower and descending into the traffic pattern, my mind bounced between air traffic control arrival instructions and frequency assignments. I was in absolute awe of what God had done, transforming Invisible Angels from a dream into actually rescuing trafficking survivors in less than twenty-four months.

The human trafficking scenario in the United States is different from what most think. First of all, *it exists*. Human trafficking is real, and it's happening at epidemic levels inside our borders. People often ask if the survivors we rescue are young girls from Central America, or immigrants trying to get into our country, or victims from Eastern Europe. Most people have no idea that the trafficking survivors we rescue and recover are American boys and girls, men and women, from ages eight to forty-eight. It's not what you see on TV; it's much, much worse.

The logistics for these rescues are crucial. There can be no downtime. We need to be in and out within ten minutes without seeming rushed or concerned. The reality is, traffickers can and will reengage, even in public places like federal airport property. Although you might not expect it, trafficking survivors can and sometimes do change their minds and go back. It's just a reality. We need to be quick, focused, and invisible.

To the best of our ability, we timed everything to the minute. Nicole, the survivor advocate from Selah Freedom, waited for us in the private terminal with Jolie, the trafficking survivor. Jolie savored her Starbucks, breathing in the aroma more than sipping it. She hadn't had a Starbucks in quite a while.

Not what most would consider the typical *trafficking survivor,* Jolie was in her late forties, bright, articulate, pleasant, and eager to leave. After a quick greeting and flight briefing, we were back on the runway in just under ten minutes.

You could think of rescues as a witness-protection program of sorts. Once separated from the trafficking environment, survivors need to vanish. To traffickers, each human life – man or woman, boy or girl – is about a $200,000-a-year commodity. That's the price of bondage in America today. Yes, it's 2025 in the United States, and these individuals, God's children, are still being bought, sold, and traded between gangs, pimps, and lone traffickers.

On this trip, we headed north, over one thousand miles away, to a wonderful safe house and rescue rehabilitation facility where Jolie would receive the care and support she needed to begin rebuilding her life.

Prayer is the core strength and lifeblood of Invisible Angels. Before any survivors see us, before any trip is planned, each survivor is prayed for from the first moment we receive the rescue request. We have a team of the greatest prayer warriors I have ever seen. You wouldn't know it by looking at them, and that is probably exactly how God wants it.

We have a woman in her eighties who has moved mountains. Another in her seventies has the power to bring heaven down to earth. A gentleman in his sixties meekly petitions for impenetrable angelic protection, and a tiny woman in her forties who, through tears, has fervently interceded for strength, peace, and protection. On every trip, we have felt the supernatural coverage of prayer. Invisible Angels would be helpless without it.

When rescued, survivors usually have nothing besides what they are wearing. So, our prayer team also puts together a backpack for each survivor filled with hygiene items, new clothes, a Bible, a journal, and a letter written by team members. I have never read the letters, but I have seen tears streaming down the faces of some survivors after reading them. I have never asked what is in the letters. All I know is that each letter tells the survivor about Jesus, His limitless love, and His plan for them. It's amazing to see the impact of God's love, grace, and holy protection on someone in such dire need of His loving peace.

We pray a lot, even while flying, and we consistently see God's hand in every journey. On every trip, once we reach cruising altitude and our passengers get something to eat, they all drift off to sleep. We couldn't ask for anything more.

Climbing to our cruising altitude, we settled in. Jolie was pleasant, talkative, relaxed, and relieved. We enjoyed the aroma of her Starbucks as it filled the cabin. She chatted with us for a while, then there were longer pauses between words. Slowly, it grew quiet, then quieter still. After a while, I looked back and saw she had drifted off to sleep. "Perfect. God, You are awesome."

Several hours later, we descended through a thin, gray, overcast sky that suggested it was colder there. After receiving our runway assignment from the center controller, we were handed over to the tower as we continued slipping through the layered clouds. Slowly, the airport came into sight, and, lining up with the runway, we floated inches above the centerline for an ultrasmooth landing. As we taxied toward the small private terminal, we saw the people from the new safe house waiting for us on the tarmac. Nicole had stayed in touch with them throughout our descent and had timed it perfectly.

It seemed we'd jumped into early winter, as it truly was about fifty degrees colder than where we'd taken off from. After all, we weren't that far from the Canadian border. As we exited the aircraft, the people from the new safe house walked over and introduced themselves. After quick hellos and thank-yous, they began to walk Jolie away; but after a few feet, Jolie stopped, turned around, and walked back to me. Looking me straight in the eyes with a heart full of relief, she softly said, "Thank you for saving my life."

She smiled, turned, and walked back, rejoining the others. Those six words froze me. I was awestruck at what God was doing, not only right in front of me but using me as well, putting me in the middle of His visible, miraculous work.

A few years earlier, if someone had told me I would start a nonprofit rescuing human trafficking survivors, I would not have believed them. That's how God works. It's hard to pinpoint when this actually began, and the actual beginning is really important. It is 75 percent of the Invisible Angels' story. Where God takes you, where He places you, and what He has to do to and through you is where the story truly begins. Invisible Angels did not begin when we acquired our airplane, or even when the idea was first planted in me two years earlier. God was at work long before any airplanes or ideas.

Several years earlier, I had lost two jobs within two years. I was in my early fifties, unemployed, and I thought I might stay that way for a while. God was clearly at work preparing me for the mountaintops while I was still deep in the valleys. That is where God does His best work: in the furnace, climbing the mountain, walking through the fire. God is continuously building the character needed to take you where He is leading you, and the character needed to keep you there.

Those valley seasons resulted in a surrender I didn't see coming. When I was in it, I didn't even notice it. It was a surrender born of sheer exhaustion and ultimate desperation. That is the place where God knows you are all His.

Invisible Angels is a story of miracles upon miracles, a season of *suddenlies* and a season of shutdowns and spiritual attacks followed by silence, surrender, and isolation. At times, the isolation was so painful I couldn't see what God was doing until pieces of me started to break off and die. Only then did Scripture come to life in John 15, with my name written on it. As each vine was pruned, trimmed, cut off, and died, I began to see what God was burning up and what He was replanting in its place.

That took time.

In Matthew 17:27, Jesus tells Peter to go down to the lake,

cast his line in the water, and look in the mouth of the first fish he catches. It was something that probably made no sense to Peter at the time, but he obeyed. He followed a seemingly inane instruction that led to a permanent miracle.

Through the journey of Invisible Angels, I have seen the same thing, except it wasn't a coin – it was much bigger. We think obedience will be hard, and it is, but we cannot limit our sight to only what is seen. There is so much more involved.

Even the smartest and most creative of us have only a single-dimensional, binary thought process. Isaiah 55:9 (NIV) says clearly, *"As the heavens are higher than the earth, so are my ways higher than your ways and my thoughts than your thoughts."*

At best, we can paint pictures, write beautiful songs, create wonderful stories, and stack bricks into spectacular cities, but we cannot make stars, planets, or galaxies. To discover and live in the will and power of God and what He has planned for us, we must obey. To obey, we must be able to hear, and to hear, we must be in His presence, and ideally, firmly in His grip. That can be a lonely, painful journey, often requiring us to do things we do not want to do to receive a prize we cannot yet see or understand, until we are well established along our new path and the silence begins to make sense.

Obedience is not about being restricted from something you want. We have to keep obedience in its proper perspective: it exists solely for our protection and preparation. Obedience ranges from keeping us safe to shattering earthly, human-based perceptions and boundaries to experience God moving in ways we couldn't dream of. What do you think went through Peter's mind when he saw the sun's reflection off the coin lying firmly in the mouth of that fish? Just imagine what he said to himself.

Thirty years later, Paul wrote in Ephesians 3:20 (NIV): *Now to him who is able to do immeasurably more than all we ask or imagine, according to his power that is at work within us.* His power that is at work within us. That spells obedience, and obedience results in more than you could ever ask or imagine. This is what I have seen, and is the story God wants to tell you.

Scripture has come to life through Invisible Angels. God has revealed His power through miracles at an unbelievable pace. Funding for each rescue appeared through prayer. The logistics, which can be quite complex, lined up perfectly, as did the people and the new relationships needed with other rescue organizations, including federal and local law enforcement. God removed people from my life and brought in others. It was, and still is, like walking in and out of a live-action prayer movie. Some days I can hardly keep up with what God is doing, and some days I have seen "the sun stand still."

We are battling an unspeakable evil. We have rescued an eight-year-old boy kidnapped by his father and put into a child pornography ring; an eighteen-year-old girl sold by her mother at fourteen because her mother needed drugs and rent money; a thirty-three-year-old woman who, after trying to escape, was the only survivor after the four other girls she fled with were murdered; and a thirty-year-old woman who had been held captive *in the life* since she was fifteen. For as long as they are held, they are raped between eight and twelve times a day, all for profit.

A few years earlier, I had no idea this was even happening. God has taken me on a journey from nothing to flying survivors to safety. Every time I tell the testimony of how Invisible Angels came to be, I keep hearing God say, "Tell My story. Tell My story."

I will. I want to tell you the story of how God started Invisible Angels and show you how God is clearly in this fight.

CHAPTER 2

DO NOTHING

Moses answered the people, "Do not be afraid.
Stand firm and you will see the deliverance the
Lord will bring you today. These Egyptians you
see today you will never see again. The LORD
will fight for you; you need only to be still."
(Exodus 14:13-14 NIV)

Most biblical miracles don't begin with parting seas or raining fire from heaven; they start with fear, confusion, and a lack of good options. Look at Moses at the Red Sea. Roughly three million people were on what should have been a two-week walk from Egypt to Israel, only to have Pharaoh change his mind and send the entire Egyptian army after them. By the next morning, probably in less than five minutes, the sea swallowed Pharaoh's entire army.

Exodus 14:13-14 are my life verses and my favorite miracle story, but the Red Sea story didn't begin with Moses being pinned down between the desert and the sea. You have to look back at the seasons that shaped Moses, the ones that taught him to keep moving forward, even when what he saw in front of him made no sense. Moses knew God would deliver him, but he did not know how. Most likely, Moses screamed Exodus 14:13-14 to the Israelites. And then, in the next breath, God said to him, "What are you looking at me for? Get moving!"

That moment at the Red Sea wasn't random. It came after forty years of military training in a palace and another forty years of wandering in the desert. Decades of shaping preceded the miracle. The parting of the sea was the result of a man who once ran for his life after committing murder, then spent four decades alone in the desert, staring at sand and listening to sheep.

Minus the murder and the sheep, my story wasn't so different. Invisible Angels began in the desert years before airplanes were ever in the picture.

In early 2003, I was a line producer for a television network and disagreed with the executive producer of the show I was working on. I was not acting in a godly manner. I may have been right, but my attitude wore thin, especially with the executive producer, who'd had enough. The show had wrapped production for the season, and it was unclear if the series would be picked up for the next season, but it was abundantly clear I would not be. Furthermore, the executive producer was angry.

Proverbs 9:7 (NIV) is well-placed here: *Whoever corrects a mocker invites insults; whoever rebukes the wicked incurs abuse.* Paraphrased, this verse is saying, Think carefully about whom you pick a fight with. Some people won't be happy that you are leaving; they want to leave a mark. And she (the executive producer) did just that.

About a week after our argument, I received a phone call from one of the network's corporate attorneys. The executive producer came back at me with the legal arsenal of the entire network. Over a trivial but very real matter, they threatened to sue me for an alleged copyright violation for hundreds of thousands of dollars. This was serious and it now had my full attention.

The lawyer on the other end of the phone was a combination of an almighty New York corporate attorney and a gunslinger dying to *get his man*. I could tell he always got his man by his tone, inflections, and attitude. He didn't lose. I could smell his cologne over the phone.

He was snarling, sharp, powerful, serious, and in thirty seconds he had scared me into financial ruin. I am sure at some point in all of our lives we have come to that realization and say to ourselves, "I can't win here. I won't last one round in the ring with this guy. I'm in deep trouble."

Admittedly self-inflicted, I was completely defenseless. I couldn't talk my way out of this, and it was clear this wouldn't go away. I immediately called a lawyer friend of mine, who was glad to hear from me. Bern and I had worked closely together several years earlier in an internet start-up, and we knew each other pretty well. More importantly, he knew me well.

As I explained the situation to him, he stopped me about halfway through. Smiling, and knowing exactly what I had done without asking for more details, he said, "Ted, no worries! Let me call them and find out where they are. I'll call you back and let you know what I hear. Just don't talk to anyone there anymore!"

God's Word is active and permanent. Hebrews 4:12 (NIV) tells us what God's Word does: *For the word of God is alive and active. Sharper than any double-edged sword, it penetrates even to dividing soul and spirit, joints and marrow; it judges the thoughts and attitudes of the heart.*

Matthew 24:35 (NIV) makes it permanent: *"Heaven and earth will pass away, but my words will never pass away."*

You do not have to act like a Christian to have God's Word apply to you; in fact, you do not even have to be a Christian. God's

Word applies to the entire universe, which He created. God's Word continuously applies to all of us, whether we know it or not.

In 2003, I wasn't close to God at all, I just thought I was. Hanging up the phone, I admitted, repented, and prayed. "God, I messed up. I really messed up. You have got to undo this. I can't fight this one. This was all my fault." Repentance is crucial; it really is the only required ingredient. I had no idea what would happen next, but I had truly handed it over to God for the first time in a long time.

A few hours later, Bern called back. "Hi, Ted. Do you have a copy of your production agreement?"

"No, I never had a production agreement."

Suddenly, it seemed Bern had a huge secret, but I had no idea what it was. Feeling his enormous grin come through the phone and almost whispering through a smile, he said, "I'll call you right back."

In a quick click followed by silence, Bern was gone. I had no clue where this was going. In a few seconds, Bern had reached a level of excitement that lawyers only know when victory is assured. I still knew nothing, but God knew where this was going. He had solved this problem long before it ever was a problem. In fact, in God's eyes, this never was a problem; it was a lesson and a reminder.

Bern called back. "Ted, they have no case. There was never any production agreement between you and the network. In fact, they sold the programs you produced to several networks overseas, and since you have no production agreement with them, you may be entitled to a share of those sales. It wouldn't be an easy case, but if you want to pursue it, I'll take it. We are talking about a lot of money."

In an instant, God turned the tables in my favor, but they had been turned the entire time. That's how He works: solving our problems upstream before we even know they exist. Our actions will always have consequences, like not getting picked up for the next season, but we are all living under Romans 8:1 (NIV): *Therefore, there is now no condemnation for those who are in Christ Jesus.* There will never be any condemnation in Christ.

Just like the Israelites' attitudes, this event was my fault, but God still had the battle won for me without it ever needing to be fought. I needed to repent, withdraw, and recognize what I did to create this, and realize and witness God's grace in solving it. I, like many, am a slow learner. It took me a while to get there, and even longer to remain still in the process. I wasn't trapped between an army, the desert, and the sea, but I was stuck between an angry executive producer and the fangs of a snarling corporate attorney comfortably seated in front of his human skull collection.

I withdrew, electing not to pursue the case, and was thankful that this issue dissolved by the end of the day. This is when Exodus 14:13-14 became my life verses. The big takeaway from this event: Do nothing. God will fight your battles for you. Much of the time, you need only be still.

Invisible Angels actually began before it was even an idea. Before any airplanes, before any dramatic rescues, I had just turned fifty and hadn't heard anything about human trafficking. I wasn't even a pilot. In fact, I was unemployed and confused. It was a season of lost jobs, lost relationships, bad decisions, spiritual warfare, the consequences of bad attitudes, the loss of my father, changing churches, and years of solid isolation.

In those seasons, we cry out to God, "Why?"

This is why.

He is preparing you. The problem is, we can't see it from where we are, and if God told you what He is preparing you for, you wouldn't believe Him. Even Moses didn't know when God told him His plan in Exodus 3:11 (NIV): *But Moses said to God, "Who am I that I should go to Pharaoh and bring the Israelites out of Egypt?"* And he had a dozen more excuses.

These seasons are necessary; they are a vital part of the Invisible Angels' story and an important part of your story. They're the bridge between who you think you are and who God knows you are.

John 15:1 (NIV) says, *"I am the true vine, and my Father is the gardener."* The loneliness, wilderness, confusion, desperation, sadness, isolation, cutting, pruning, and disciplining are God preparing you for what He has planned for you, and it is much bigger than you think!

We all want an off-ramp when things get tough. The challenge can come when God asks you to tithe, and you take that vacation instead. Or when you feel the Holy Spirit nudge you to give up your first-class airplane seat for the elderly woman in the wheelchair, and you refuse. Or when God removes the relationship, job, or person in your life who is not bearing fruit, and you fight Him on it.

Those are the moments when we usually take the exit to the *highway of my way* because we are usually solely focused on avoiding the discomfort. What we cannot see is what hangs in the balance by not being obedient.

God's plan for you hangs in the balance.

This is the case with Invisible Angels. If you were to hold a Christian measuring stick up to my life, I would be completely unqualified and undeserving to be anywhere near this mission. But that's the beauty of it – we are all unqualified. And yet, I have seen God's grace, peace, and kindness in rescuing trafficking survivors, and I am bewildered that I am the one He chose to do it through.

I am absolutely amazed at how He has woven together every part of my life: my passions, interests, desires, failures, talents, previous jobs, my regrets – everything. I have read stories like that, heard testimonies like that; I have studied them in the Bible, but nothing could've prepared me to see God move like this in real time, over and over again.

So let me tell you how it all began.

CHAPTER 3

PRUNING

"He cuts off every branch in me that bears no
fruit, while every branch that does bear fruit
he prunes so that it will be even more fruitful."
(John 15:2 NIV)

The year 2013 was a year of pruning.

I was in a comfortable government job that I loved, producing multimedia English-teaching content for a global audience. It was fantastic. I worked with an incredible team, and we were producing super-creative teaching programs. We had a blast at work and created a fantastic product that the entire world enjoyed. We had over 1.4 million monthly users, and I was knocking it out of the park. Our whole team became very popular. I won a few awards, which are meaningless now, and I achieved higher visibility. I thought I was untouchable.

That's when the real trouble began.

In government, senior leadership can change instantly. People retire, new people are appointed, and others simply move on, up, or out. In the blink of an eye, someone new can be placed over your entire division, and they don't care who you are, they don't care about your past success, and they certainly do not have your best interests at heart. They have their own.

This is precisely what happened.

A few floors above my office, a very short meeting took place in a fancy conference room I rarely visited. I was not invited, informed, or involved. A colleague and I had heard about the meeting, which was to announce a significant management appointment that directly affected us. We decided to sneak into the back of the conference room and find out what was going on. In ten seconds, it was done: I had a new division director. And just like that, he appointed someone new over me. In less than a minute, my entire work landscape had changed.

Over the next few months, everything my team had built over the past few years was being dismantled in favor of what my new boss wanted, regardless of our past success. I quickly went from being the division superstar to a contestant in an office version of *Lord of the Flies*. Government and any corporate environment can be that way.

The working environment worsened over the next few months. The stress built to an unbearable crescendo. I couldn't believe how quickly things had changed. I had never experienced anything like this, and it was affecting my health. This was instantaneous, like turning a corner directly into a lion's den, except I wasn't Daniel; I was a wounded baby gazelle.

Coming from an entrepreneurial background, I had no idea how to navigate this. To make a bad situation worse, I wasn't handling it prayerfully at all. The Enemy was having a field day with me. Not even consulting God, I made it worse by using earthly weapons and failing at every turn.

Nothing is worse than a hostile work environment; in government, one must be uniquely shrewd and a skilled politician to navigate this landscape. I possessed none of those talents. I did not get along with our new director, and my new boss and I were on even worse terms. I was slowly dying on the vine, and then, to finish me off, the director started making moves toward my termination.

Things can change fast. It is very hard, if not impossible, to fire someone in government, even with cause, but they can make your life so miserable that you will resign.

That was the strategy.

I wasn't connecting with God because I wasn't praying. I knew He saw me struggling, and even though the root cause of this was self-inflicted, I knew He was still with me. However, I didn't have the spiritual maturity or the scriptural knowledge to pray my way through this nor out of this. I just didn't realize that at the time. The stress hit an unbearable level, and then it seems God decided I went through enough.

At the height of the struggle, on an evening when I was so glad to be home but sitting there dreading the next workday, the phone rang. It was my friend Lorraine. We had worked together on a documentary a few years earlier, and she had just become the vice president of communications at an association in the DC area. These are very sought-after, prestigious jobs. She needed to put together an all-star digital media arm for this association and asked if I would be interested in leaving my secure, comfortable government position and leading this new team.

She had no idea of my current work situation, and I can't tell you what a relief it was to get this phone call. Before I even had time to process it, she offered me the Director of Digital Strategy and Operations position. It came with a significant salary bump, a great title, and what I thought was my divine escape hatch.

I proudly thought, "Surely this must be God."

Glorious Christian victory music ran through my head all

night and throughout the next day. Visions of God rescuing the Hebrews consumed my thoughts as I walked into the office the next morning, wearing a smile that hid my secret: "God has seen my plight and my struggle, and He has answered my prayer! I shall soon be leaving all of you, stepping onto God's new victory path for my life. I shall soon be leaving all of you to suffer under this twenty-first-century Pharaoh."

The only thing was, I never really prayed about it; I just complained, and what was about to happen was anything but an answer to prayer. It was a setup for a serious life lesson.

I met with Lorraine and the association's leadership the next day, and that evening, over a phone call, I took the job. Without thinking about it, without praying about it, without consulting any Christian brothers, mentors, or elders in my life, I just jumped in. It was a rescue from a horrible work situation that had come right in the nick of time. Unexpected and unannounced, this appeared to be a complete and total answer to all my problems.

I left the government job, along with all the benefits and retirement, packed up my office, handed over my computer, and signed out. I had a feeling of victory, like I had won the battle. Fueling my pride, I thought, "This is God rewarding my brilliance! I was right the whole time. I am out of here! Thank you, Lord!"

Turns out it wasn't God. Just a few months later, they fired me.

Six months later, and in just under two minutes, I went from a big-shot director to an unemployed fifty-one-year-old with two mortgages, a boat, and many other things to pay for. My ego, or what was left of it, needed to be mopped up off the floor. Probably just the way God wanted it.

Welcome to the world of executive-level jobs. It doesn't matter if you are right, smart, or know what needs to be done. You are shown the door if you are the wrong fit and they don't like you or what you are doing. No hard feelings, no drama, just big-boy, big-city reality. The job was just a wrong fit. I was just the wrong guy for the post. They gave me a severance package, which I had to fight for a little, and we amicably parted ways.

Now, I had a new title: officially over fifty and unemployed.

From my new vantage point, the government job I'd left looked much better. "Maybe I should have stayed and ridden it out." There, I had left a solid retirement plan, security, and a good, high-paying job to chase the *executive track*. I took an off-ramp out of a bad situation, and I had a small feeling – one I tried to ignore – that maybe God wanted me to stick it out in the government situation and pray my way through it.

It didn't matter now; I had a new adjective to deal with: *fired*.

My church life was good. I had been in the same church in Maryland for over ten years, and was firmly plugged in. Friends reached out, and, as God would have it, some friends were fired from their jobs around the same time. Classic Christ-irony. We encouraged and reminded each other that God never wastes a wound.

Emotionally, I was on top of the firing. I wasn't depressed. I had more experience as a freelancer than as an employee anyway, so this didn't scare me. I knew what to do. I just felt like an unemployed over-fifty loser. I knew how to get freelance work that actually paid better and was fun to do.

After a month or so, I reached out to a friend at another government agency to see if they had any contract work available. She was pleased to hear from me and immediately said, "Well, I have something that may be quite cool. It's overseas."

"Cool! Where? What are the details?"

I am always up for an adventure, but not like this one turned out. The country? Let's just say no one puts it on their travel bucket list. It wasn't exactly a vacation spot. But I leaped at the chance!

The job was teaching aviation-English and developing materials for their air force pilots on their base. This particular air force was participating in a NATO exercise, but most of their pilots could barely speak English, if at all. All their pilots had to pass an International Civil Aviation English-language exam so their country could participate in this exercise. We had to get them to pass that exam. That's all we were told.

This was a big deal, working in cooperation with the State Department, the military, and NATO. My friend said I was a perfect fit. I had spent the past eight years building English-speaking multimedia content and absolutely loved aviation. I had even started my pilot training numerous times over the years, though I never finished. Instantly, I thought, "Clearly, this must be God!"

It certainly was, but not in the way I expected.

This turned out to be one of the most terrifying episodes of my life. It could have ended very badly. Again, without praying or consulting anyone, I jumped at the opportunity, hopped on a Boeing 747-400, and off I went.

It was a ten-week assignment in a spiritually dark place far from home. The country, though, was absolutely beautiful. It had an incredible culture, immense mountain views, and breathtaking landscapes. But spiritually, it was heavy.

I did not walk with God while I was there. No daily reading, no quiet time, no prayer life to speak of, nothing. The job was easy, and I treated it like a vacation in a wildly different place. I had friendly relationships with all the pilots. But the culture? Totally different. There were also many moving parts to this contract that I did not know about.

We had an American military liaison officer watching over us. He was our general contact, and for the ten weeks we were in this country, we were to contact him if we needed anything. We met him when we first arrived, had dinner with him a week or so later, and never heard from him again.

Now, let me explain *how* we were even there. International government-contractor travel can get tricky. We were in-country on tourist visas as American civilians teaching aviation-English to their air force pilots on their air force base.

No one briefed us on safety. No contingency plans. No emergency contacts. No US embassy contact. We were basically on our own. A couple of weeks into the project, it hit me: this could go very wrong. International government work can get very complicated if you are not working under a diplomatic visa, especially if you are working with their military on their military base. You do not have American law to protect you.

By week nine, the end of the contract was coming up, and I was really looking forward to going home. I remember lying in bed a week before my departure date, thinking, "I would love to go home today."

Guess what was about to happen.

The previous day, two colonels came into the computer lab to talk to me as I was getting ready to leave for the day. They struck up an odd conversation with me. They started trashing America. They launched into a rant, in their thick accents, that the United States was filled with liars, was completely immoral, and that the news media was completely out of control.

Two thoughts entered my mind: They were pretty much right, and when did their English get this good?

They continued. "CNN can say whatever they want! It's all lies. American society is trash, and your government lies to the world. You live in your big houses, driving your fancy cars. It's all a lie!"

The intensity was jarring. This went on for a few minutes, and they weren't really wrong.

I smiled and said, "We have a free society. We can say anything we want. We can publish anything we want; that's America. We have free speech, and that's the core of our society. You have to take the good with the bad."

They left, and they seemed angry. I had a good relationship with these two colonels the entire time I was there, so I was a bit confused about why they would come in and unload like that.

After they left, I brushed it off. I didn't give it much thought – until the next morning.

The military liaison officer had given us cell phones to use in-country. I never used mine, but we were to keep them with us at all times in case he needed to contact us. Suddenly, mine rang in my backpack. I answered, and it was the liaison officer, screaming at me.

"You had a conversation with the colonels yesterday? What did you talk about? You cannot talk about American policy on this base; you can't have conversations like this! Why did you even talk to them? You have jeopardized this whole operation!"

In a full military rage, he screamed at me for another two minutes. I had no idea what he was talking about. My conversation with the colonels was of no value, or so I thought. What operation? What was he talking about?

That's when the lack of a diplomatic visa hit me like a rock.

Still shouting, he barked, "Report to the base commander immediately!"

Now I was worried.

I went down the hall to the base commander's office – someone I had met several times. He was very nice, polite, and a professional military officer in his mid-thirties, but he did not look or sound like he belonged where we were. When I first met him, I thought he was from Texas. He had a polished Latino look, was good-looking, and smooth. He had a good sense of humor and spoke perfect American English. I didn't think it was that odd, since many foreign military officers are educated in American universities.

As I walked toward his office, the word *operation* kept ringing in my head. Connecting the dots of not working under a diplomatic visa, I realized I may have stumbled into real trouble.

Knocking on the door to his office, he greeted me warmly, invited me in, and asked if I would like a cup of tea. He was very calm and nice; his mood was completely opposite that of the screaming military liaison officer.

He told me that my conversation with the colonels the previous day had shown up in his daily report. Yes, a daily report.

Pouring my tea, he said, "Ted, we can't have conversations like that."

He went on to explain the country's policy and the military policy regarding *conversations of this nature*.

This was surreal. I didn't know what was happening. Sipping my tea through slightly trembling hands, I apologized. "Colonel, I am deeply sorry. I thought it was a regular conversation; I didn't know I had done anything wrong."

He agreed and understood, but he wasn't finished. "I know, Ted, but I have to act."

Then came the hammer.

"In a few minutes, a white van will arrive that will take you back to your hotel. We need you to pack up your things and go directly to the airport. We have a flight for you out tonight."

A few seconds of awkward silence ensued.

He held my gaze, then smiled. "Please, finish your tea."

I was stunned, frozen.

He offered to write me a recommendation letter, saying I had done a great job, but had to be removed. He could not have been nicer. Now I seriously started to wonder if my tea had been poisoned. This happened so fast that I did not have time to think.

Then the white van arrived.

The colonel shook my hand, walked me to the van, and off I went.

In less than ten minutes, I'd gone from a normal day to wondering if I was being hauled off to a secret location to be *reeducated.* My head was on a swivel, staring out every window of the van to make sure we were going back to the hotel. What if we weren't? Where would they take me?

I slid my hand into my backpack and wrapped it around my cell phone. My finger hovered over the redial button in case I needed to call the screaming liaison officer. Would he even answer? I was on a tourist visa!

For the next ten minutes, I was terrified.

Then we turned a few familiar corners. As the hotel appeared at the end of the street, I released the cell phone back into my bag. This was starting to feel like a spy movie, and I had no idea how it would end.

Once back at the hotel, I had about fifteen minutes to pack my things. The liaison officer called me again. "Your airline ticket is at the front desk."

It was. I never spoke to him again.

I caught a taxi to the airport, and about twenty-eight hours later, I landed at Dulles International Airport, relieved and happy to be home, but bewildered at what had just happened.

There was no record of my removal; it never appeared on any government security paperwork, and I was paid the full amount as if I had completed the entire contract.

To this day, that entire episode is one big question mark. I was just sent home, and I was very happy to be there.

I was profoundly confused. What happened? I had been fired from one job and then released from another within a matter of months. Everything in my life seemed upended; nothing seemed stable. No one knew I was sent home a week early, and as far as anybody knew, the whole *getting sent home* episode never happened.

However, a very close friend, intimately familiar with that part of the world, completely understood what had happened. She said, "It's how that part of the world operates, and you were lucky to get out of there. Don't think about it anymore. Just move on; you have a great story to tell."

I did just that. I chalked it up to a great story, another great adventure, and settled back into being home. Now I just needed another job.

In Washington, DC, you can always find contract work as an eLearning developer or multimedia producer. If you find the right projects, they can pay very well, and some have a relatively short project timeline (three to six weeks), which is great; when they are over, you move on to the next. Manage these projects and clients well, and you'll have a very good work-life balance.

That's what I did for several months. I stopped chasing work, and it just appeared. I stopped forcing things and trying to be someone with a title or a global English-teaching platform, and I just worked. I was hired to create awesome projects. I created wonderful courseware for a large cellular company, did a lot of smaller video work, which I truly enjoy, and a lot of narration or voice-over work, which is easy. Suddenly, I had much more time to spend with God.

At the time, I lived about forty-five minutes outside Washington, DC, on the Chesapeake Bay, out in the country. I loved it.

I started working from home and realized the empty space God was creating in my life – empty space to spend more time with Him. Without the grind of a three-hour commute to and from work, I had a lot of empty space in my day.

Throughout the rest of 2014 I had no problem finding work. I was working almost entirely from home, and I was busy. Oddly, aviation eLearning and multimedia development became the running theme; aviation projects just kept popping up. I took a longer-term contract at a wonderful aviation-related company and thoroughly enjoyed working for them. Working there was peaceful. As that contract came to a close, I started scanning www.Indeed.com for my next project. On a Monday morning, I got online, and the first eLearning developer job that popped up read something like this: "eLearning developer / multimedia producer needed with current aviation-related content experience. Preferably ten-plus years of experience in eLearning authoring tools. Please reply with links to work samples."

No company mentioned, no address, no phone number, and no person. It simply had a "reply to" email address.

In Washington, DC, this was not surprising. Many government agencies and private firms do not put their names on job ads for security reasons. These are usually very cool jobs. This time, I didn't scream, "Clearly this must be God!" I had a feeling it was, but this was different; it was a breadcrumb, an open door. I quietly walked through it and sent my resume in.

A few minutes later, I got a response with an attached zip file and a simple message: "Please follow the directions in the 'read me' file."

DC at its finest!

I opened the "read me" file. "Please use the attached materials, images, video, and content to create an eLearning course with a final exam. You have two hours from the time you receive this email. Thank you."

I love stuff like this. This was actually very easy. They supplied all the content; all I had to do was put it together.

I designed a clean, sharp template, with an awesome font choice, added a nice narration track, a beautiful music bed, and even polished their graphics a bit. I thought it looked really nice, and I sent it in, made lunch, ran a few errands, and by the time I got back to my desk, I had an email from the nonreply email address: "Thank you for your submission. Would you be able to come to [discreet Washington, DC address] tomorrow at 10:00 a.m.?"

I replied, "Yes. I look forward to seeing you then."

As I drove into the city the next morning, I racked my brain to think of who or what might be at this address. A quick search turned up nothing online, which isn't surprising in DC. Only government office buildings are in that area, and the only one I thought it could be was NASA, which was right around the corner.

I found the nondescript, cool-looking building, went up to the second floor, and saw the name etched on the large double-glass doors: Lockheed Martin.

Seeing the name sent an electric shock wave through me. On the other side of those doors sat the best aerospace company in the world. Civil and military aircraft, rockets, spacecraft, and everything else in between, I was staring at almost a century of aviation and aerospace ingenuity, and one of the best companies on the planet. People lined up to work there, and I was walking through those doors by invitation.

I registered with the receptionist, was given a visitor's badge, and was greeted by a tall, well-dressed, sharp-looking woman. Though in civilian clothes, she introduced herself by her rank. "Good morning, I'm Sergeant Mitchell. Nice to see you. Please follow me."

I instantly liked her, while simultaneously being terrified of her. Using rank worked. From her demeanor, she meant business. For this interview, every word that came out of my mouth had better be thought through, spelled, and punctuated correctly. She wasn't there to be charmed.

I sat down in the chair in front of her desk. She opened her computer and started typing . . . and typing. For at least five minutes, she was just typing. I quietly sat there. This was probably the longest time I had been quiet in front of someone since the winter of 1963, when I was born.

She kept typing. Finally, she looked up and smiled.

I thought it might be safe to say something then. Holding my iPad, I said, "Would you like to see my eLearning samples?"

Without looking up, she said, "No, I already have."

I just smiled.

She continued typing. Then, about thirty seconds later, I said, "Is there anything you need to know?"

Smiling back, she said, "No. I have everything I need."

She stopped typing and looked at me in a matter-of-fact, no-big-deal kind of way and said, "Oh, you're hired. Can you start tomorrow?"

"Yes."

"Great. Go down the hall to the security office, second door on your left, and they will take care of you. I'll see you tomorrow at 9:00 a.m."

That was it. I didn't do anything to get hired. I didn't even say a word. I just showed up on time, well-dressed, and ready to go.

This was Lockheed. People take pay cuts to work there. They don't take people off the street like this. It was so clear that God had just opened a new set of double doors for me to walk right through. It was also clear that God was sending me back to school.

Lockheed had a great culture. I felt that from the moment I walked through the door. I was hired as a contractor to develop eLearning courseware and multimedia for the Federal Aviation Administration (FAA). I don't know why they kept that so secret, probably just policy.

Right away, I created courseware on everything from servicing and replacing runway lights to pilot compliance with regulations and recurrent training for air traffic controllers. I loved every course I worked on. I loved being a contractor as well. There were no benefits, but there was better pay and greater flexibility in terms of time and telework, which gives you a far better work-life balance. This was an awesome job.

Lockheed Martin was filled with current and former military personnel. Every manager and director I encountered was either a colonel, lieutenant general, or general. Not including my recent overseas experience, I had never worked in a military environment. I felt very comfortable there.

I liked the crystal clear direction and objectives. No nonsense and absolutely no games. It was an environment where you excelled and were recognized for your performance. They had informal "awesome people of the month" awards where, in the monthly all-hands staff meetings, they would give out an informal award, usually a coffee mug, a T-shirt, or a selected piece of Lockheed paraphernalia, to an individual who did an awesome job. From the receptionist to the contractors, all were included. It was very informal, but also real and effective. Titles didn't matter. They treated everyone with the same respect, regardless of employee or contractor status.

It was very clear that God was gifting me this job. My role? Keep my mouth shut, do a good job, and do exactly as I was told – three things I had a problem doing in the last few years – well, honestly, since 1964. This had been a blind spot for me my entire life, and now God was gently making me aware of it.

Being at Lockheed was different. I had a sense of reverence for the place and the people I worked for and with. The colonels and generals did not care about new ideas, better methods, or creative flair. They just wanted it done well, on time, and according to contract. It was very simple. There was always something very cool going on there.

As God would have it, overnight I was in a completely new place and at the beginning of a new season.

In God's loving way, He was teaching this fifty-two-year-old much-needed discipline. He gave me an awesome place to work, but to really thrive, I had to behave and follow the rules. I did so, not out of fear of losing my job, but out of reverence and obedience because I respected my coworkers, and I loved it there. The more I obeyed, the better my life became.

A few months in, I realized, "What incredible irony!" This is exactly how we should be and where we should be with God! We must obey Him with a healthy dose of reverence and complete obedience driven by our love for Him. The more we obey, the more peaceful and purpose-driven our lives become, and the closer we get to Him.

God taught me this in an environment I loved, with healthy but firm boundaries and no condemnation. Only God could do that.

Throughout the fall and winter of 2014, I settled in. My work and church life were good. I had played in worship bands for years and played in my church's worship band almost every week. I was hitting a new, peaceful stride. At the same time, I became a bit quieter and more still. I started listening for God out of sheer desire because I wanted more of Him. This season slowed me down. Way down.

Over the past year, I had seen God move me through two bad situations: losing one job and being removed from another. I also realized that, for me to move on, give it to God, and let things go, I had to do my part and take responsibility for the bad situations and consequences I had created.

God wove that truth in and around me gently, without condemnation, and provided gentle course corrections along the way. Most importantly, I listened.

The more I listened and obeyed God, the closer I became to Him. My strongest lessons in obedience were through tithing. For the first time in my twenty-five-year walk with Him, God's Word became alive and active, sharper than any two-edged sword.

God had me in a place where I was listening and wanting more.

I also wanted more out of the church I had been a part of for the last twelve years. We had started as a church in a box, hungry for God's Word, hungry for discipleship, and fiercely bound to creating a new community. Sure enough, within twelve years, we had grown into the large community we were striving for.

We started as a handful of trailers and volunteers, setting up church on Sunday mornings in an elementary school, and became a twenty-four-acre campus with a beautiful building, soccer leagues, and after-school and weekend sports programs. We became a large part of the local community and drew people in because of that.

Our worship band grew bigger and better. We became more professional, got better equipment, and became more polished. Our worship practices became more prayer-focused as well. This caused all of us to take a closer step toward God and really center and focus our purpose for being part of the worship ministry. All of us felt that.

As 2014 drew to a close, I found myself entering a new and different phase of my life. I was coming up on fifty-two, and I really wanted to trade the things I was doing for myself for things I could be doing for God.

I have always leaned forward into life. I have lived overseas several times, seeing parts of the world few people ever get to see. My career has been diverse, ranging from a special-education teacher to a television producer to a seasoned multimedia producer. Part-time, I had been an actor, an improv comedian, an offshore bareboat coastal navigation sailing instructor, and crewmember on yacht-racing teams in Annapolis. I was even a yacht broker for a few years.

I have always been wired that way. If I'm interested in something, I don't just talk about it, I do it. That is how God made me, but now life was becoming less about me.

Around this time, I said a life-changing prayer. I didn't plan to say this prayer; I didn't even think about it. But when it came out, it carried unexpected weight. While at a worship-band practice, I remember silently saying to God, "Lord, this next season of my life is Yours. I have done everything I wanted to do. You take my life from here."

I said this out of desperation, but not the panicked kind. It was more of an "I am out of ideas," which I was. After twenty-five years of walking with Christ, I could not, and should not, manage my Christian walk. That is God's job.

This prayer settled me. Again, I didn't plan it; it just came out. Soon after, I felt God saying, "Finally."

Over the next few weeks, a new peace came over me. Things at Lockheed were going well. I was leading a small group at church, and my desire for God was growing with a strength I had never felt before. It came out of a sheer desire to know Him better.

For the first time in my Christian walk, I started hearing His voice at a new level.

In January 2015, in worship-band prayer time, while everyone prayed the usual worship-team prayers, I silently, mentally, and prayerfully stepped away. I asked God a question He had been waiting for me to ask for the last twenty-five years: "Jesus, what do You want from me this year? What do You want me to do for You?"

Instantly, I heard God say, "Do nothing."

This is when things really started to happen.

CHAPTER 4

GOD THE RESTORER

"I will repay you for the years the locusts have eaten—the great locust and the young locust, the other locusts and the locust swarm—my great army that I sent among you." (Joel 2:25 NIV)

Restoration can come through a circuitous path.

At Lockheed, I fell into a groove. Without any effort of my own, I found myself being asked to join other projects and lend my expertise in certain areas. I quickly became part of a great instructional design team working on some very high-level projects.

At the time, there was a big-budget, high-visibility project that had gone sideways. I wasn't working on it, but I had overheard the issues in office conversations. These issues started out small but were left unchecked. Of course, over time, they grew worse. Whenever "The Project" came up in office conversation, the problems were bigger and more serious. I had an easy fifteen years of experience on most of the other team members, but I never gave any advice, because I was never asked to. God told me to be still, silent, and "do nothing." Plus, I was still terrified of Sergeant Mitchell.

I had a lot of respect for the design team I was with. They were all amazing, great, and creative designers and developers, but from the overheard conversations, The Project was not going to end well if it could be completed. A few days later, on a Thursday afternoon, an email popped up: "Ted, Lt. Colonel Alexander wants to see you. Now. – SGT. Mitchell."

Lieutenant Colonel Alexander was responsible for a whole series of contracts at Lockheed. Brilliant, organized, and extremely disciplined, he was a true leader in every sense of the word, and in my ever-expanding Pixar Studios animated thought life, Alexander had his own theme music as he walked down the hall. He was a retired lieutenant colonel in the United States Marine Corps. He was all Marine.

Although I spent little time with him, I always called him The Colonel. He was one of the reasons I loved Lockheed. Straight to the point, no nonsense. Be brief, be bold, and be gone. Just as Sergeant Mitchell brought me in on that first day, every word that came out of my mouth had better be pronounced, spelled, and punctuated correctly.

I had no idea why he wanted to see me, and I knew I wasn't in any trouble, since I had been keeping my mouth shut all year. This new, self-imposed silence grew into a new sense of peace I was unfamiliar with, but it was extremely welcoming, especially in instances like this. Within a minute, I was still and silently seated in a chair in front of his desk.

"You needed to see me, sir?"

"Yes. Ted, 'The Project' could use your expertise. I need you to join the team, and we need to deliver this project on time and on budget, without any issues."

"Yes sir."

"Thanks."

That was the longest conversation I ever had with Lieutenant Colonel Alexander. Once I joined the team, got into the details, and started attending meetings, I realized this was a complete mess, the worst I had ever seen. Everything had gone sideways. Everything that could go wrong did, and it spun out of control without supervision. Sometimes this just happens. Large-scale contracts can be tricky. Contractors are usually focused solely on completing the project and usually have a blind spot regarding the politics and personalities involved.

That's a big deal on the client's side and is usually irrelevant to the contractor. Also, large-scale multimedia projects are very similar to large-scale construction projects. It costs $1.00 an hour to change things in the planning and design phase. It costs $100,000 an hour to change things once they have been built. Add in explosive personalities, squabbling government employees, and too many people involved, and things turn into a mess that no one catches until it is completely out of control.

The wrong people were selected to lead this project from the beginning, and although they were fine, skilled individuals, it wasn't working. The Project had to be completed and delivered by the end of the year, which was coming up quickly, and at every turn, there would be a major derailment, and we would be right back to where we started.

This was God's new training ground for me: get in, don't get involved, don't give your opinion, just demonstrate your solutions. I knew exactly how to do that; I had just never done it. Plus, I had a new *fear chain* in my life: God, Sergeant Mitchell, and Lieutenant Colonel Alexander, in that order.

I had a healthy fear of God, but Sergeant Mitchell and Lieutenant Colonel Alexander were right down the hall, and I could see them. A little bit of fear, pointed in the right direction, can be an excellent motivator.

When you listen to God, you can see the possible on the

horizon when you are surrounded by the impossible. My job was simply to deliver this project by the deadline. How did I start? By doing nothing – nothing out of my own will, just simply doing the job.

During my time on The Project, I had many frank, opinionless conversations with the client. I did nothing in those conversations except state the facts. I had no dog in the fight and nothing to gain. I just did nothing. I was not being lazy or avoiding work; I was just staying focused on only what I was asked to do, something that most of us learned in fifth grade, except I was absent that day. The client appreciated my candor.

I just gave them an honest, opinionated assessment of everything. This built up a tremendous amount of goodwill. The Project was delivered on time and on budget, and then something even bigger happened.

Just by my showing up, doing my job, listening to God, and "doing nothing" else, I had earned a new reputation as a seasoned professional who can bring a team together to get something done and be counted on to be frank and honest. This lesson resulted in a permanent attitude change, grounded in gratitude. The still-fresh unemployment episode, followed by the "white van ride of terror through the dark streets of the unnamed city," was still a fresh memory. I was so thankful to be working at the best aerospace company in the world.

We must remember to view our circumstances from the perspective of God's blessings followed by God's instructions. Do nothing.

Shortly after The Project was delivered, I received a phone call from one of the leaders at Lockheed. "Ted, I wonder if you would be interested in working here full-time as an employee, not as a contractor."

This was truly amazing, but after discussing the details, the pay was far below what I was making as a contractor. Although

I didn't think they intended to be insulting toward me, it was surprising how low the offer was. I politely declined, but the experience was incredibly positive and motivating. If they were serious, they would come back.

Barely a few days after the offer, and maybe this was the reason for the offer, an email arrived containing two words every contractor dreads: budget cuts. Overnight, people were gone. That's contractor life. They wanted to keep me around, which was a really big deal. I made the short list at Lockheed Martin, but there was a catch. They needed to move me from production to budgeting, something I wasn't thrilled with, and I would have to be in the office every day – no more teleworking. This was a big-enough deal for me to consider walking away from Lockheed altogether.

Walking away would have been tough, and probably not a good decision. I loved it at Lockheed, and I was building a good reputation, but on the other hand, there was no work-life balance. I wanted to keep my newfound peace and sanity that I had working from home. I simply got more done. There were no interruptions. I could be more creative, work faster, and I needed the silence. Returning to the office would mean returning to a three-hour round-trip commute, on good days. I was about to turn it down, and then I heard God say, "Do nothing."

Do nothing, as in, don't even decide. Don't react. Follow the breadcrumbs. See where this leads. I felt God saying, "I have something for you here, but you'll only see it if you follow Me."

I took the job: creating production budgets for online course development. I had been in the entrepreneurial space for over fifteen years prior to working in government, as a television producer, and running our own eLearning production and development company. Prior to that, I was involved in an internet start-up. All I knew was the entrepreneurial space, since I had left teaching in 1995. I knew exactly what the costs were. The problem was that this work would be boring.

Again, I heard God say, "Do nothing."

Excel spreadsheets are anesthesia, and staring at numbers paralyzes me. In college, I failed accounting three times, and my instructor only passed me on the third try because she knew she wasn't doing the world any favors by keeping me in basic accounting for three semesters. But I listened, and I leaned into what God was doing.

For the next few months, it seemed as though nothing was happening. But it was. I was asked to help out on a few projects here and there, and before long, I was being brought into higher-level meetings because of my development experience, all while God was telling me to "do nothing." The more silent I became, the more would happen.

On Monday, one of the Lockheed managers popped his head into my cube and said, "Ted, a team downstairs could really use your help. Could you spend a few weeks working with them? They could use your expertise, and you could probably get them squared away quickly."

Down a floor I went and met the team. They were wonderful, and we instantly clicked. After meeting with them several times and getting into the details, I discovered they had done all the heavy lifting; their project just needed to be organized, cleaned up, have graphics applied, and be delivered.

I enjoyed working with this team; we all got along very well. Over the next few weeks, there were more and more conversations about future projects, how much they needed someone with my skill set on their team, and how much fun we had. All I did was show up. Nothing I did, no effort of mine, put me in this position; I was just quiet, obedient, and still. And God being God, the God of blessings and restoration, our God who wrote through the apostle Peter in 1 Peter 5:10 (NIV), *And the God of all grace, who called you to his eternal glory in Christ, after you have suffered a little while, will himself restore you and make you strong, firm, and steadfast,* did the moving and the shaking.

God was about to split the Red Sea wide open again, but slowly this time.

I answered the phone in the middle of the workday, parked in my small carpeted cubicle. Someone asked me for something that I can't even remember now. We started talking. To this day, I can't remember why he called or who he was, but we began laughing about shared experiences in government work life. He seemed like an awesome guy. We laughed about office episodes that were taken right out of *The Office* television show or could have been its inspiration. I told him I had been in government previously and left to take a private-sector job that didn't work out, and now I was back as a contractor. Then he made a comment that would instantly change my future.

"Do you know that if you were to be hired back into the government within two years of leaving, all your benefits and service time would be reinstated?"

"Really?"

"Yes!"

He stated the exact policy and where I could find it on the Human Resources web page. Scanning through the page, the paragraph jumped off the screen.

"Wow. Sure enough, it's right there! Hey, let me take you out to lunch!" I said to him.

Explaining everything over lunch the next day, something I didn't even think was possible was now a reality visible on the horizon. If I were to be hired back into government service within two years of leaving, all – and I mean all – of my service time would be reinstated. Obviously, I didn't have thirty years, but what I did have was significant. Now, all I needed to do was get a job offer from the government. I had three months.

Right around this time, I had a family vacation planned to the Outer Banks of North Carolina. Just a week in early winter when the beaches are deserted, the tourist shops are closed, the temperatures cool down, and the entire area is delight-fully abandoned. On the first day, while running to the store for supplies and getting settled for the week, I passed a sign for discovery flights at a local flight school. Squeezing the brakes to a quick stop, I backed the car up to the side of the road. I stared at the sign.

With wide eyes, images flashed through my mind of the hundreds of model airplanes I built as a kid, the middle school book reports I wrote on *The Aircraft Engines That Won World War II,* and the dozens of *FLYING* magazines I hoarded in my room, reading the same stories over and over, and my eternal love of aviation. And there it was; it popped back up again.

I remembered my dream. The only thing I ever wanted to be in life was a pilot. My pilot's license had eluded me since I was sixteen. For various reasons, from becoming a derailed teenager to not having the funds and focus in later years, here I was, at fifty-two, staring at a sign that asked me one question: "Would you like your dream back?"

I started my pilot training when I was sixteen, then in my twenties, then in my thirties, and again in my forties. Each time, I never finished; life got in the way. Flying is something you have to be all-in on. You can't do it part-time. Most importantly, you need time and money to get your pilot's certificate. Now I had both. God had placed me between the greatest aerospace company in the world and the federal agency governing all things aviation, the FAA.

Sometimes we don't see what God is weaving together until it's completed, staring us right in the face. Silently, looking at the sign, I answered, "Yes, please" to the thirty-six-year-old question. I called the number and told them I'd be there in an hour.

Arriving at the flight school, I immediately met an extremely enthusiastic flight instructor who happened to be the owner. I told her about my previous flight experience, and in thirty minutes, I was in the left seat of an airplane taxiing toward the runway. From the moment the engine started, the hopeful, beautiful, amazing smell of Cessna exhaust screamed, "Today, you get your dream back." I was all-in and committed.

I had no idea what God had in store for me.

Coming back from my vacation week, I was working and walking on a cloud for the next few months. Learning to fly while working at Lockheed and the FAA was a surreal experience, and I could not have been in a better place. Everything I did, worked on, or came into contact with obviously had something to do with flying. Everything was always lining up. The entire team, and even management, was very supportive of me getting my pilot's certificate. Surprisingly, there were not that many pilots in my division.

Even as a student pilot, I was now in the air, talking to controllers and landing at a variety of small to medium-sized airports. Surprisingly, I was the only one in our department doing so, which gave me an entirely new, fresh, and extremely useful perspective at work.

Still working with the new team, our project was coming to a close, and they kept asking about my future availability. "I am wide open; just clear it with Lockheed."

They were about to do one better.

Michael was the manager of the group I was working with. With a joyous attitude, quick with a joke, always smiling and always positive, he was fun and safe to work for. Michael was very protective of his people and treated everyone excellently. A former air traffic controller, he was always a few steps ahead of the team. He was one of those few people with that natural ability.

The phone rang on an ordinary day, back in my government cubicle. It was Michael.

As I answered, he practically shouted, "It's a good day to be Ted!"

"Hey! I like where this is going! How are you?"

Whenever I talked with Michael, I always expected a punch line, but I never knew when it would come. I had to stay sharp with him; I never knew where our conversations were going. This kept me guessing and it maintained an *on my toes* attitude at all times. Trying to keep up with him was futile; I usually fell far behind within minutes. He was brilliant. This conversation was no different.

"Hey, I've got something I want to talk to you about. Do you have a minute?"

"Sure. I'll be right down."

Making my way down the floor, I was in his office within a minute. Popping into his office, I sat down, and, with a smile, he said, "You want a job?"

Without skipping a beat, though smiling, I said, "Yes, please."

I thought he was kidding, but he wasn't. This could have been a scene from *The Office,* except that Michael was serious. He spent the next ten minutes talking about how this would be the shortest job interview he had ever given. He had watched me interact with the team over the last few months, had seen the product we produced, and there was no question in his mind that I was the right fit. Michael offered me the job, and I immediately accepted. He said he needed to get the paperwork started, but the process should go pretty quickly since I was previously in government service and my security paperwork was still current. After twenty minutes, we were done.

As I was walking out, he said, "Oh, by the way, get your pilot's license."

That comment could have only come from one person, and He has been knitting this story together the entire time. Sudden and complete restoration.

About 2,900 years ago, the prophet Joel delivered an encouraging prophecy in Joel 2:25 (NIV): *"I will repay you for the years the locusts have eaten—the great locust and the young locust, the other locusts and the locust swarm—my great army that I sent among you."* God will restore the years the locusts have eaten, even if you were the one feeding them.

God will use the valleys to shape, mold, and discipline you. Read the verse again. He was the one who sent the locusts to begin with. If you turn to Him with a sense of urgency and repentance, God will restore you.

Joel continues in 2:26-27 (NIV): *"You will have plenty to eat, until you are full, and you will praise the name of the LORD your God, who has worked wonders for you; never again will my people be shamed. Then you will know that I am in Israel, that I am the LORD your God, and that there is no other; never again will my people be shamed."*

With eight weeks to spare, I was sworn back into federal service. My retirement and health care benefits were restored, and, as an extra bonus, I was brought in at a higher grade level, earning more than my previous government position and more than I earned as a contractor. By the end of 2016, I had a job offer from an industry giant, a new reputation, a new playing field, full restoration of my government service and retirement, a pay raise, a fresh spiritual education, a new attitude, and my dream of becoming a pilot – all while doing nothing. And I had no idea what God had planned for me next.

CHAPTER 5

I NEED YOU TO BE OF SOBER MIND

In their hearts, humans plan their course, but the Lord establishes their steps. **(Proverbs 16:9 NIV)**

Proverbs 16:9 offers a quiet but profound truth. It lays out an overview of how God orchestrates our paths.

We have passions and desires, usually the things we are best at. God weaves those together to fulfill His will through us. The alignment of our heart's passions and desires with His will results in His will being achieved through us. The catch is that we usually have no idea what that entails.

On a beautiful, cold North Carolina winter morning, my enthusiastically bold flight instructor slammed the cockpit door shut. Barely five-foot-three, but with contagious energy that could lift the wings on its own, she began the briefing for today's flight.

"We are going to continue perfecting your basics today! You're going to take off, climb to five hundred feet, make a ninety-degree left turn, continue climbing to one thousand feet for about a quarter mile, level off, make another ninety-degree left turn, and follow parallel down the runway. When you get to the middle of the runway, drop a notch of flaps, bring your power down, turn on the carb heat, and start your descent to eight hundred feet. About a quarter mile past the runway, make another ninety-degree left turn, drop another notch of flaps, watch your power, and descend to five hundred feet. Make another ninety-degree left turn, line up with the runway, drop the rest of your flaps, adjust your power to stay on the glide path, and land. Once you land, don't stop! Turn off your carb heat, raise your flaps, apply full throttle, take off, and repeat."

It's called pattern work, and it masters takeoffs, landings, and the basics of flight handling. After a few laps in the pattern, we left the airport, climbed to three thousand feet, did some steep turns over the beautiful North Carolina coast, made a few landings at a nearby airport, and headed back home. It was simple.

After landing at the home airport, we were taxiing back toward the hangar, and I thought I was done for the morning, but the Holy Spirit and my flight instructor had other plans. She was about to set up an encounter that would change my life. As if she were mad, she barked, "Stop the plane here!"

What did I do wrong? silently ran through my head. Startled and practically slamming on the brakes, I stopped the airplane, and as I went to shut down the engine, she blocked my hand.

"No! I want you to do a couple of laps in the pattern . . . without me. It's time to solo!"

Jumping out of the airplane and slamming the door shut, she ran a little more than a wing's length away. As fast as she jumped, she stopped, turned, and stared back at me. As I looked back at her, eyes and mouth wide-open, she cracked a huge smirk, pointed toward the runway, and waved goodbye. Every student pilot is terrified at this moment because they never think they are ready, and if they are cautious, they shouldn't be overconfident. But she knew something I didn't: I was ready.

Terrified, I taxied out, turned onto the runway, applied full power, and was off, by myself. Rolling down the runway, my fear increased with my speed, but the instant the airplane left the ground, I felt a holy peace come over me. My nervousness dissolved as I started my first lap in the pattern. Everything was perfect.

Completing the final turn and lining up with the runway, I was about to make my first solo landing. *A deep breath in, get yourself about one foot above the runway, level off, pull back on the power, and wait until you stop flying.* With a gentle fade onto the runway and no bouncing, I nailed it! My first solo landing!

Applying full power and rolling down the runway, I lifted off again and went for another lap. As I made the first climbing turn for lap number two, an unmistakable invisible cloud of peace began to fill and consume the inside of the airplane. I was still flying, still in control. I still heard the engine, but now the Holy Spirit had entered the airplane.

It felt like a faint hint of angelic music behind a series of thoughts that weren't mine, being live-streamed into my mind. But it wasn't a text crawl like on the news. All the words were there at once, except I didn't have to read or hear them. They were simply there and understood, all at once. It was just peace, permanence, and strength. Speaking without words, the Holy Spirit began . . . .

"This will be the next season of your life. You have always dreamed of becoming a pilot, and now you will. You will be flying, using aviation to help people. You will be serving; just keep moving forward. Follow Me."

The Holy Spirit stayed in the airplane while I was flying. I can't tell you how many laps I did in the pattern, but there was such peace and permanence to every takeoff and landing, and they were all pretty much perfect.

God unveiled a new season to me as I continued to land and

take off, circling the pattern repeatedly. There were no details, just breadcrumbs. He would reveal the next steps in pieces as I followed His direction. It was all I could handle at that moment, because if God had told me the entirety of what He was about to do, I would not have believed Him.

Landing the plane and taxiing back to the flight-school hangar, I kept my Holy Spirit experience to myself. I knew that no one, at that moment, would understand, but now God's desires and my path were beginning to align. That had never happened before.

"'*Your kingdom come, your will be done, on earth as it is in heaven,*'" from Matthew 6:10 (NIV) is a key verse and a very well-known Scripture, but we often do not look under the hood at this simple request. Matthew 6:10 is a request for alignment: God's will to be done on earth as it is in heaven. It is asking for God's predetermined, eternally existing, perfect, and prede-signed will, just for you. Heaven will come down to earth when our lives align with His will. Heavenly-earthly synchronicity.

It was God's will all along that I become a pilot, not at six-teen but at fifty-four. God knew all the *whys* that would end up determining the *whens.* It still happened; I became a pilot, and God had timed it for His purposes, so when it did happen, I would bring a lifetime of experience into this new season.

Matthew 6:10 can also be seen as a starting point. When your path aligns with God's will, you will know it. You may not have a holy cloud engulf your airplane, living room, or car, but you will have a specific, majestic, confirming peace that originates from deep within your heart's desire. It's where God's will aligns with your desires and direction.

This started to happen to me.

Pouring through every area of my life, I heard from God like never before. He was consuming, loud, and clear, so much so that the valley seasons were now making sense. Now those seasons began to reveal themselves from the perspective of God's love instead of what I thought was a punitive season of discipline. As I stepped into the path God had prepared for me, I watched Him direct my steps. My work life began to align with God's Word in every aspect, largely because I started to respond to people and circumstances with Scripture taking the lead rather than my own thoughts and ideas being at the forefront. The more I turned to God, the more peace I had.

The key was one simple step: read a chapter of Proverbs daily until a proverb comes to mind in response to any situation. *The wise store up knowledge, but the mouth of a fool invites ruin.* Proverbs 10:14 (NIV) is my *work verse,* and it has saved me from a lot of trouble, and actually, earned me a few promotions.

As I continued through the remainder of my flight train-ing, the right people, projects, and materials supporting exactly where I was in my training would just land in my lap. If I was studying for the navigation portion of my FAA written exam, a navigation-based media project would pop up in my inbox. While I was doing my cross-country flights, safety media would be needed for airports I had recently flown into and out of. I felt God's direction, protection, and peace so strongly during this time. Just about everything in my life was aligning with the path God had for me.

During this time, God led me to a new church filled with a fresh, hungry group of believers and fantastic, Bible-based, Spirit-filled teaching. Overnight, I was fed in ways I hadn't been in years. I began attending men's groups and Bible studies, and I was thrilled with their energy, digging deep and teaching the Word. There was an amazing peace about this change. Everything felt aligned. It was exactly where God needed me to be.

With a new church came new Bible studies and new friends. It was refreshing to be surrounded by new faces all seeking the Word. God was beginning to lay the framework for a new foundation I desperately needed. He began to prepare me for the season and the arena I was about to enter, and I had no idea the size of the demonic giants I would face in the next few years.

God did.

Be alert and of sober mind. Your enemy the devil prowls around like a roaring lion looking for someone to devour. First Peter 5:8 (NIV) lays out a basic warning for all, and describes the Enemy's primary offensive strategy. The results can be found in the first half of John 10:10 (NIV): *"The thief comes only to steal and kill and destroy; I have come that they may have life, and have it to the full."*

The Enemy comes only to steal, kill, and destroy. During my albeit new and brief involvement in human trafficking rescue, I have seen what the Enemy has done to God's children. Peter's *lion* doesn't begin to explain the destruction that traffickers have inflicted on helpless and defenseless human lives.

During the 1990s, I spent about six months in West Africa. Lions generally stay away from people; it is the crocodiles you have to worry about. Lurking just below the surface of the water, invisible but fully locked onto you, crocodiles burst upward out of the water in a fraction of a second, jaws wide and merciless. Before their prey can even flinch, their powerful jaws clamp down with over two thousand pounds of pressure, crushing it instantly.

As their jaws close, the crocodile spins violently, not in circles, but along its longitudinal axis, like a drill. Eighty-plus razor-sharp teeth shred flesh and bone in seconds. Then, just as quickly as it began, it is over. The crocodile drags its prey slowly back down to the riverbed, disappearing under the water.

A lion may represent how the Enemy stalks his prey – waiting, watching. But a crocodile shows how the Enemy strikes – suddenly, silently, ruthlessly.

If you are entering any type of ministry, take 1 Peter 5:8

seriously. But don't just watch the grasslands, watch the water-line as well. The Enemy lies in wait, beneath the surface, ready to pull you under the moment you lose your focus.

Depending on your ministry, your spiritual life as well as your physical life may depend on it.

You need to be fully prepared, which begins with hearing the Holy Spirit, who is the Spirit of truth and provides all the primary guidance you need. You must be able to hear, access, and obey the Holy Spirit at all times, because it is the foundation of your Christian walk: powerful yet profoundly sensitive.

Luke 3:22 (NIV) sets the tone: *And the Holy Spirit descended on him in bodily form like a dove. And a voice came from heaven: "You are my Son, whom I love; with you I am well pleased."*

The Holy Spirit is also sensitive – very sensitive. Throughout the Bible, He is symbolized as a dove, and with good reason. In Scripture, doves represent peace, purity, love, humility, and new beginnings – all the stages God will take you through if you surrender.

To hear the Holy Spirit, my spirit needed calm and rest. I was nowhere near that. For most of my life, I had been consumed and distracted. My spirit was buried with static, hurry, chaos, anger, noise, drinks and distractions, and the many other spiritual obstacles that have infected my life, blocking the Holy Spirit's voice from my spirit, rendering me unable to hear Him.

You don't realize it's happening until it has already happened. Jesus spent a large amount of His time in solitude. Luke 5:16 (NIV) tells us how He spent His time: *But Jesus often withdrew to lonely places and prayed.* My guess is He absolutely needed to. His earthly ministry must have been constantly surrounded and badgered by chaos, anger, division, backstabbing, greed, selfish desires, lust, murderous thoughts, and everything else in between.

Think about this: Jesus' spirit was from heaven, a place of

absolute peace, where there is nothing that hinders peace. Jesus was also the one who wrote the law with His finger on Mount Sinai. There He stood, millennia later, in His beloved city of Jerusalem, arguing with the Pharisees and Sadducees, who had turned God's loving guidelines for comfortable obedience into a warped interpretation of civic regulations and social procedures. They had taken the law far from its original intent.

We live in that same world, except we now have cars, Wi-Fi, cell phones, and the Kardashians, making the static far worse.

This is why many are unable to have a relationship with the Holy Spirit and, unfortunately, can never understand Him. Most of the time, these spiritual obstacles are self-inflicted. In my case, all of them were. To make matters worse, I wasn't even aware of this; it was a blind spot. To even begin to create a relationship with the Holy Spirit, I needed to stay close to and in the Word to recognize any gaps in my spiritual walk.

That awareness only comes from a place of stillness, quietness, peace, and a true longing to be closer to God and learn who He is. I was just starting to get there. As airplanes were climbing, my life was quieting down, and God was rising up. I was decreasing, God was increasing. It was noticeable.

God had started laying out His vision for me as I was in new Bible studies, a new church, and was being challenged in and by the Word for the first time in years. To keep that spiritual path open and growing, one obstacle had to be removed: alcohol.

I come from a long line of alcoholics. From ages ten to seventeen, I rarely saw my mother sober. The good news is that it only took one time for my mother to finally hit rock bottom. She came out of rehab in 1979 and earned thirty-two years of sobriety. She never drank again. She achieved a well-earned eternity in glory in 2011. My mother's sobriety was her greatest achievement and a model for anyone facing a sober life. She, by the power of the Holy Spirit, was able to maintain her sobriety with a perfect record for over three decades, but as anyone will tell you, there was rarely an easy day.

My father, although I rarely saw him drunk, was a drinker and remained one until he left us in 2019.

My maternal grandmother was a heavy drinker, and from what I understand, so was just about everyone on my mother's side of the family, going back as far as 1635, when our ancestors began keeping family records. Alcohol was always present in our lives, slowly and simultaneously destroying us. We just never saw it until it was too late.

My dad and I always enjoyed having drinks together. We talked about my mother's victory over alcohol quite often, usually over drinks. We always said we (my dad and I) had an off switch, but my mother didn't. What I didn't see was that my off switch was a dimmer switch.

In my twenties and thirties, I drank quite a bit. Always controlled, I never craved a drink during the day, never drank at work, never had to hide my drinking, and never needed a drink; so technically, I was fine. But I was still drinking a lot. I drank less as I hit my forties and then my fifties, but now a glass of wine or other drinks seemed to hit me harder. Alcohol became more powerful and affected me differently. I cut way back and enjoyed a glass of wine with dinner, and really enjoyed a bottle with friends here and there, but something was different. Looking back, I had no idea how alcohol could outrightly block the Holy Spirit from speaking to one's life.

I was in a new season. I had a new job, was becoming a licensed pilot, had a new church, was meeting new friends, and new friends meant a new future. I also had a new mission. As this season took deeper root, I began to yield more and more. It was inches at first, but as time went on, I felt God stripping me of things I loved. I was strangely happy to let these things go. It was like throwing away old clothes or decluttering – freeing and refreshing. My previous priorities were evaporating and being replaced by this new season.

Sailing, which was my identity for over forty years, wasn't even a remote interest anymore. I have been around boats, sailing, and teaching sailing my entire life. For over thirty years, I have had many large sailboats, and I even lived on my boat, on and off, for ten years. I raced sailboats on various racing teams in Annapolis and up and down the Chesapeake Bay.

Annapolis has been described as a town filled with alcoholics who have a boating problem. I was part of that crowd. In 2015, I suddenly sold my thirty-seven-foot Gulfstar sailboat. I was just done. I was losing interest in the sailing lifestyle, which was centered around what was on sale at the liquor store and how fast we could load it onto the boat.

I still had many sailing friends, but now I wanted to let that whole group and chapter of my life go. After walking with Christ for over thirty years, God was louder and clearer than ever before. The more I gave up, the closer I felt to Him, and the more focused I was on this new season.

Annapolis evenings in the fall are beautiful, especially on a boat. Fifty-nine degrees, air so crisp you can take a bite out of it, brilliant-colored sunsets streaming through the masts, the ringing of the rigging slapping against the masts, the smell of leaves and wood-burning fires all permeate the air.

I loved Chesapeake sailing in the fall. It finally cools down enough to be comfortable, and there is consistent wind! On a typical fall Annapolis Friday night, I popped over to a friend's boat for Friday evening margaritas at a restaurant close by. As we got to the table, the first round was dropped off, and as I brought the margarita to my mouth, just before I took the first sip, I heard God's gentle voice in my spirit: "For what I have prepared for you, I need you to be of sober mind."

Without taking a sip, the whole room suddenly fell silent,

though everyone I was with continued talking as usual. The restaurant's audio had just been muted, at least in my mind. This split second seemed like half an hour. It was the Holy Spirit, and I was the only one hearing Him. At that moment, I knew He wanted me to stop drinking, but I didn't think my drinking was that big of a deal. What happened next was more like an "Aw, come on," similar to what a child would say when asked to put their iPad down at the dinner table. "I thought I wasn't drinking that much. It wasn't a big deal," I answered back, with an undiagnosed level of hubris. "Besides, I like a Cabernet with a steak." Pretty gutsy to talk back to God while having only arrogance to offer in return.

He repeated Himself: "For what I have prepared for you, I need you to be of sober mind."

With the table still silent, a veil was removed. Instantly, I saw everyone at the table as being foolish, spending their time in a foolish manner. Then the script was flipped. It dawned on me that this was not my time for myself, but God's time for me to spend with Him – His time, which He had planned and prepared for me. I couldn't waste it. Proverbs 13:20 (NIV) rang through my head: *A companion of fools suffers harm.*

And then I heard Him say, "Leave."

"What will they say? How can I just leave?" I was sitting inside the booth, too! That same gentle voice simply said I didn't need to be there any longer.

He said, "Just tell them you have to go."

I did just that. "Hey guys, I have to go."

I didn't even touch my drink. I put it back down on the table the moment I heard God speak those words to me. My friend and his wife just said, "Okay." It wasn't awkward or anything. I just left.

I don't really remember leaving the place, but I do remember the drive home. I was stunned. I heard from God, and after a very short Q and A, I obeyed. I felt so free. I also remembered that I didn't have to worry about being pulled over, and then the thought popped into my head: Nothing will end your piloting privileges faster than a DUI. "For what I have prepared for you, I need you to be of sober mind" was repeating itself over and over again on the drive home and for the next several months.

That night I started hearing from the Holy Spirit and God like never before. I never announced that I had stopped drinking. It wasn't an issue until my inner and outer ten-year-old childishness popped into the picture.

A few weeks later, I went on my monthly visit to see my ninety-year-old dad in Tampa. He was in great shape, driving and dating. Jumping into his convertible to go out for dinner, with his thirty-year-old attitude and a brand-new car, he roared backward down the driveway while focusing only and intently on the monitor in the center console. He had his own unique, nerdy, academic-scientist level of cool.

We got a table, and he ordered his usual: a twenty-eight-degree chilled Tito's, straight up with a twist. I thought, "Well, I am certainly not with a bunch of fools; I can have a glass of wine." After all, I am with my dad. As I took my first sip, it was different. It felt wrong, like I was letting God down. I felt an instant separation. I ignored it, and my dad and I had a great dinner and a great time. I thought it couldn't hurt, and it was only this once.

Sometimes when we ignore God, there may be no instant consequence. He may be giving you time to figure out the importance of what He is trying to show you. For me, this time, God was serious.

I believe in angelic encounters, and I have had several. Hebrews 13:2 (NIV) tells us what to expect: *Do not forget to show hospitality to strangers, for by so doing some people have shown hospitality to angels without knowing it.* Scripture is filled with these stories. They are all real. I have seen angelic encounters in my life, even when I was an unbridled teen, and I have listened intently to other people's angelic episodes.

They are all real; however, we think angelic stories are usually all nice. A benevolent angel suddenly appears and rescues you, illuminating something, separating you from something or someone, or even stopping time for you. Some stories can be very nice, but make no mistake, angels mean business because they are about God's business.

The next night, my dad and I went out again, this time to a nicer restaurant. Since I had done so the night before with no consequence, I thought there would be no harm in having a few drinks again with my dad over dinner. The glass of wine arrived, and then dinner. My dad and I would always play a unique, originally created intellectual history game over dinner and drinks. He usually went first. "What if Kennedy lived?" And we would continue through many other historical hypotheticals, proceeding down that road, rewriting history.

This was my favorite conversation game with Dad. We loved talking through events, redefining history, reshaping the world's problems, and then realizing, usually over a few drinks, how incredibly simple it is to solve these problems if only they had thought like us. It always ended up being a very enlightening, fun, and wonderful conversation, but usually, only for the two of us. The glass of wine turned into glasses, and, from the looks on our table neighbors' faces, we were becoming a little loud and obnoxious.

In the middle of our conversation, I noticed an odd couple walk into the restaurant. The man was very tall, well over six feet, maybe even seven. He was pushing a woman in a wheelchair. He looked to be in his late sixties, maybe early seventies, and he was . . . well, he was ugly. He looked like Lurch from *The Addams Family*. He wore a dark suit, glasses, and had blond hair. His presence was instantly felt.

I assumed the woman in the wheelchair was his wife. She had blond hair, and I don't remember seeing her face. They moved toward a large round table in the middle of the restaurant, but something about it struck me as odd. The table had no silverware or plates, just a large black tablecloth draped over it. The restaurant was very nice and crowded, typical for a Saturday night. For a second, I thought it odd that on a Saturday night, the largest table in the restaurant lacked silverware and plates, and honestly, I couldn't recall ever seeing that table there before.

I continued playing the conversation game with my dad and laughed at something he said. As I laughed, the tall man turned around – deliberately. His turn was noticeable. There was a force to it. Power. Silence. He locked eyes with me, and without warning, he shouted, "I told you to stop!"

It was loud, but no one else seemed to hear it. His voice hit me like a fire hose of ice, straight to the core. I froze. There was gravity in the scream I still can't explain. I knew right away it was angelic, and I knew God meant business. I was in trouble. The ten-year-old boy whose mother told him not to do something a hundred times, and who still did it, had just gotten caught.

Consumed with the feeling that I had done something really wrong, I looked down and didn't make eye contact with him. I was afraid, but my dad didn't notice anything. He went on with the conversation. It appeared as if he didn't see the event. I jumped back into the conversation with my dad, only a little quieter this time, and I didn't want to make eye contact with anybody. Again, it was odd that my dad did not notice or mention the event.

I remember feeling afraid to show my face in the restaurant because I had been yelled at in public. I was engulfed by that embarrassing feeling you get when you have done something foolish in public; but nobody seemed to notice. A few seconds later, the tall man and the woman in the wheelchair were gone.

I don't remember seeing them leave. They were just gone. This scared me, as it should have. I didn't ask my dad if he had seen the event; I knew he hadn't. I knew who the message was from, who it was for, and how serious it was. I haven't had another drink since that moment.

We serve a God of second, third, fourth, fifth, and sixth chances, but we cannot take advantage of those chances when we know better. I do not believe God's grace runs out, but I do believe His warnings do. This was stark and severe for me. Alcohol needed to be removed from my life entirely. It was. This also opened a new level of obedience for me, a level of obedience necessary to see the next series of miracles God would begin laying before me.

CHAPTER 6

A SEASON OF MIRACLES

So Abraham called that place The LORD Will Provide. And to this day it is said, "On the mountain of the LORD it will be provided." (Genesis 22:14 NIV)

When God decides to start a ministry, He doesn't start with your strengths, but with your surrender. You will likely have nothing: no resources, road map, or qualifications that make sense on paper. Everything required to launch, grow, and maintain the ministry will seem just out of reach – intentionally so. Why? Because that's the exact place where God shows up. He will produce the miracles, do the impossible, and get the glory. If this doesn't sound logical, open your Bible to Jeremiah 32:27 (NIV): *"I am the LORD, the God of all mankind. Is anything too hard for me?"* That Scripture will prepare you for what God has prepared.

From January to May 2017, my Friday afternoons looked the same. Around 3:30 p.m., I would grab my backpack and my yellow Lab and make the four-hour drive to Manteo, North

Carolina. I loved every second of my training, and working at the FAA gave me an additional layer of education that money couldn't buy. I took advantage of every imaginable resource at my fingertips, and with dozens of pilots, air traffic controllers, and other aviation professionals a mouse click away, I was surrounded by wise counsel.

Getting your pilot's license is not hard, it is just hard work. Flying the plane is the easy part. The challenge is understanding weather and atmospheric conditions, engine operation and performance, weight and balance, aerodynamics, navigation, and most importantly, aeronautical decision-making. All of this must be fully understood.

It's not just passing a test. Although you only need a minimum of 70 percent to pass the exam, you also need a medical certificate from an aviation medical examiner, ensuring you have no serious medical issues, clearing you to fly. That medical requirement would come back to threaten my wings a few years later.

You must also accomplish key operational milestones: solo basic flight maneuvers, takeoffs and landings, go-arounds, a solo cross-country flight of at least 150 nautical miles, recovery from stalls and unusual flight attitudes, basic dead-reckoning navigation, the use and understanding of basic flight instrumentation, and diagnosing engine emergencies in flight. Proficiency in all these areas must be demonstrated.

After completing a minimum of forty hours of flight instruction demonstrating proficiency, you are then signed off by your flight instructor and proceed to your final step: a check ride with an FAA-designated pilot examiner. Separate from your flight instructor, the designated pilot examiner (DPE) is usually unknown to you. They are independently contracted by the FAA to sign off and approve new pilots and current pilots with new ratings. Your private pilot check ride has two parts:

an oral exam, lasting usually over an hour, and a flight component where you must demonstrate full proficiency in all flight
maneuvers. For new pilots, these flights can be nerve-racking.

Just imagine: you have completed all your flight training,
spending thousands of dollars and weeks, months, and sometimes years all on a ride, haunted by the image of some evil
government overlord watching your every move, waiting for
you to fail. This is not the case at all.

The FAA has done a wonderful job of making your private
pilot check ride feel like your first flight with your first legal
passenger. Most DPEs have a gentle spirit and want their candi-
dates to pass, and most do. If an instructor signs off on a student
before they are ready, however, the spotlight shifts back to the
flight instructor. They do not risk that. If they send unprepared
students, they will not be flight instructors for long. Aviation is
built on a deeply ingrained safety culture that works very well.

On a very hot Saturday morning, check ride day arrived.
I buckled myself into the little Cessna 150 and flew the two
hours to the middle of nowhere in North Carolina to meet
Greg, my DPE. The little Cessna 150 only cruised at ninety
miles per hour, so I had my window open the entire way. It
was a fun flight and great preparation. Talking with air traffic control the entire time, I was routed around arriving and
departing aircraft and some random glider traffic. I requested
a few altitude changes to get into some cooler, smoother air. I
was relaxed and confident when I landed at the small airport.

Then I realized I had forgotten my lunch. I was starving.

Walking into the conference room, I shook hands with Greg.
He must have sensed an anxious mix of hunger and student-
pilot nervousness, and in his calm voice, he said, "Would you
like to go out to lunch? I haven't eaten yet."

"Absolutely. I'd love to!"

God had this all prepared. The first portion of my oral exam took place over pizza. It didn't even feel like an exam. We spent about an hour at the airport covering navigation, airspace, weather, and regulations in the airport's small conference room. It was material I had been studying for the last five months and was already a part of my daily conversation. The conversation ended with, "You really know this stuff," and a slight smile indicating I had passed. But it wasn't over.

Next, was the flight. This was a simple flight with my first legal passenger, who would be asking me to perform flight maneuvers I had been practicing for the last five months, except that this flight got off to a terrifying start.

Weight and balance are crucial in aviation. Whether it's a Boeing 777 or a small Cessna 150, an aircraft cannot exceed its maximum designed takeoff weight. If it does, it will not fly. As part of the check ride, I had to prepare a weight-and-balance equation for myself (180 pounds), for Greg (150 pounds), 144 pounds of fuel, and 50 pounds of bags and other items in the back of the aircraft. The useful load in a Cessna 150 is 580 pounds. With little room left, we were extremely close to maximum takeoff weight.

Temperature affects aircraft performance. If it is hot and humid, your aircraft will have greatly diminished performance. It was well over ninety-four degrees that day. Rolling down the runway, slowly gaining speed, the aircraft became airborne, but something was wrong. It felt enormously sloppy, like I was flying an overweight cow. It was climbing too slowly. The normal climb rate for this aircraft is around 350 to 500 feet per minute; at best, we were only climbing 100 feet per minute. Straight ahead, the trees at the end of the runway were coming right at us at sixty-five miles an hour. Here I was, heading into trees about forty seconds into my check ride.

My mind went into hyperdrive. I couldn't increase the climb rate; we would stall and fall out of the sky. Surrounded by trees on all three sides, there was nowhere to turn. I began mentally calculating our angle of climb to see if we would actually clear the trees, now closing in fast, about 800 feet in front of us. "What am I doing wrong? Engine power and temperatures are good, RPMs are good; what on earth is the problem?"

Then, in a calm Southern drawl, as the trees were closing in 200 feet away, Greg looked over at me and said, through a smirking grin, "Do you like to climb?"

Then it hit me. With the trees approaching fast, I looked him over from the left seat, thinking, "There is no way this guy is 150 pounds! He is more like 180!" The last time this guy was 150 pounds, Jimmy Carter was president. His *reality weight* of 180 pounds brought the aircraft right to maximum takeoff weight, which is why we were climbing so slowly, and it being a hot day made the climb rate even slower. Still within safety parameters, it was just very uncomfortable when we flew over the trees at about fifty feet.

I had two answers to his "Do you like to climb?" question at that moment. Either it was a simple "Yes," and continue with the flight, or "Are you really 150 pounds?" which would have initiated a prompt return to the airport and a *failure* on my check ride. Choosing the wiser option, I kept my mouth shut. I just looked at him and smiled as the trees passed behind us and we slowly climbed up to cooler air, slowly increasing our climb rate as we began our flight.

I took Greg for a ride through the beautiful North Carolina countryside, with the windows wide open, as I ran through all my maneuvers. It was seamless, fun, and not at all stressful, and as fast as it began, it was done. A few hours after I landed back in the middle of nowhere, North Carolina, my lifelong dream was slid across the table to me on a government form FAA-8060-4: Temporary Airman Certificate.

With my handwritten name and freshly inked signature, I was

now officially a pilot. Starting at sixteen and earning my pilot's certificate at fifty-four gave me thirty-seven years of life experience, immensely increasing the value of what I had just accomplished. Again, God knows all the *whys* that determine the *whens*.

As I flew home, with the windows wide-open, government form FAA-8060-4 was folded in half, tucked neatly inside my flight bag. This was now the most valuable thing in my life, not because I had finally earned it, but because God's timing had ordained it. This is exactly when He wanted me to become a pilot.

Since my solo, visions of an aviation ministry continuously exploded in my head. I didn't have any details, just the idea, and I wanted more. *What will it be, God? What will I be doing? A missionary pilot in Africa? An air ambulance pilot? What is it? Tell me!* Digging a little deeper to get the answers, this grew as a slow crescendo from a craving to an insatiable hunger.

For the next year, I found myself planted at a wonderful, Spirit-filled, Bible-teaching church just outside of Annapolis. With dozens of life groups, men's groups, and Bible studies to get involved in, I was suddenly part of a whole new Christ-loving community, all eager for the Word. Like skipping a couple of grade levels, I was thrilled at actually being taught and challenged at church, and most importantly, just going. I wasn't in the worship band; I wasn't behind the scenes; I was just attending, and I loved it. I had been with the same Bible study group for the entire year, and there was actual learning going on. We all became comfortable sharing everything from personal stories to struggles and everything in between. That's how groups grow.

The year 2018 was an extremely divisive year for the group, however, and no one knew it was about to get worse. Even as some minor arguments broke out, heated discussions turned political, ugliness reared its head, and some even got angry and stormed out, but no one ever permanently left the group.

I watched John 13:34-35 (NIV) come to life: *"A new command I give you: Love one another. As I have loved you, so you must love one another. By this everyone will know that you are my disciples, if you love one another."*

This verse doesn't say we have to agree with one another; it says we have to love one another. It's a command! If someone doesn't agree with you, is it really going to change your life? Does it matter? Are you so important and always right? And here is the big question: What would it look like to lose the argument?

We can all learn from one another, even if somebody believes Elvis and Michael Jackson are alive and well and living in a mobile home in the New Mexico desert, taking orders from Bill Gates to control the weather. Most importantly, if we all share what God is doing in our lives, we can see what an incredibly dynamic and loving God we have who meets each of us individually, exactly where we are.

People in our Bible study obeyed and applied John 13:34-35 to their lives. Even in the midst of and after disagreements, apologies were made, eyes were opened to new viewpoints and perspectives, and we all gathered again for a celebratory dinner. That's growth! It was a very comfortable place, the perfect place to learn about and see God's Word come to life, and exactly the environment God would use to start a new season.

The year 2018 was also the year I fully exercised my rights and privileges as a private pilot. Within weeks of earning my pilot's certificate, I bought into an airplane partnership and crisscrossed the DC, Maryland, and Virginia area, as well as making quick trips to Florida and Wisconsin for air shows and fly-ins. Digging into the vision God had given me, I got involved with an aviation ministry in central Florida, completing flights throughout the southeastern United States and even Central America. That first year, I accumulated just over three hundred flight hours.

The airplane partnership I had bought into complained that I was using the plane too much. "Fine," I said. So I bought my own airplane and flew even more! Still feeling God's call and purpose for an aviation ministry, although I hadn't heard anything specific, I kept following the breadcrumbs, just flying and leaning into the Word for the entire year.

An unannounced guest speaker popped in on our regular Wednesday night Bible study. She was from Maranatha Freedom, and I had no idea what Maranatha Freedom was, or what she was there to talk about. All nine of us, comfy in the living room, drinking our assorted fancy teas, welcomed our new guest. What she said over the next forty-five minutes changed the course of my life, completely taking over and resulting in lives being saved and beginning a season of miracles, as outlined in Ephesians 3:20 (NIV): *Now to him who is able to do immeasurably more than all we ask or imagine, according to his power that is at work within us.* I couldn't even begin to imagine what was about to happen. She sat down on the side of the couch and began.

"I want to talk to you about sex trafficking in the Baltimore and Washington, DC area."

For the next forty-five minutes, she went on to describe the sex trafficking industry and activity in the Baltimore and DC area, as well as the surrounding suburbs. I had never heard of sex trafficking being a problem in this country. I knew it was horrible in other countries, but surely not here. Not in America. I thought she was exaggerating the issue for the first ten minutes, maybe even making some things up. But as she went on, her facts lined up, and her details were too precise to be false. Then it dawned on me: she was telling a true story.

I was horrified, truly horrified. This would keep me awake. This issue drilled deep inside me that evening and wouldn't leave. It was as if God had hammered a lead pipe right down the center of me. I remember driving home thinking, *This can't possibly be happening.*

I don't know why this hit me so hard. I was a special-education teacher from the late eighties to the mid-nineties. I have a heart for people who get left behind, but this was Auschwitz-level -trauma. Absolutely unspeakable. I didn't realize the impact this had on me at the time, but God had dropped this inside of me like a bag of wet cement that began to harden.

When I got home that night, my friend Kelly called just as I walked in the door. I immediately jumped to this question: "Hey, have you ever heard anything about sex trafficking in this country?"

"Oh! Yes! I just finished a book by Christine Caine called *Undaunted.* It's all about how she started her organization, A21, to raise awareness and money to fight human trafficking. I'll send it to you."

Kelly went on to talk about how bad the problem was in this country, and I was stunned yet again. I always thought I was pretty current on social-cultural issues, both good and bad. I found myself completely clueless on this subject.

Two days later, the book *Undaunted* arrived. I only made it through the first forty or so pages. I had to stop reading. I was horrified. God had dropped another wet bag of cement inside of me, and as this one started to harden over the next few weeks, it began to grow cement roots. I wasn't able to stop thinking about this. Something was different, and I knew this would be with me for a while.

As the next few weeks passed, I thought of ways to volunteer or get involved. At first, I thought I could help out with multimedia production, maybe in video or eLearning production. I hadn't really put aviation into the equation yet. I found myself searching online for human trafficking organizations that were involved in the rescue, recovery, and rehabilitation of trafficking survivors, and then I came across one that stuck: Trafficking Hope.

Pastor Lee Domingue, from Birmingham, Alabama, founded the organization. I stumbled upon a sermon he gave to Hope City Church in Houston. Trafficking Hope was involved in the rescue, recovery, and rehabilitation of survivors, and they partnered with other safe houses and rehabilitation facilities. After listening to his message, I was impressed by how well-organized and well-funded they were and, above all, how Christ-centered they were. Then a question occurred to me: "Once these survivors are rescued and removed from their environment, how are they getting to safety? They obviously have no ID and are in no shape to navigate an airport. I wonder if transporting trafficking survivors using private aircraft would be a need?"

I called them the next day.

The next day happened to be the day for an FAA agency-wide meeting in a beautiful, brand-new Department of Transportation building just off the waterfront in Washington, DC. I can't remember what the meeting was about, and I really didn't care. That morning, all that was on my mind was calling Trafficking Hope and learning more about their operations.

I stepped out into the shiny new hallway during a break and called them. A pleasant, eager voice answered the phone. Throttling into the conversation at about six hundred miles per hour, I wanted to know what they did, what their needs were, and how one could get involved. About ten minutes into the conversation, with a big smile, I said, "Look, I don't know if this is necessary, and if you think I'm crazy, just let me know, and I'll let you go."

I felt a smile come through the phone.

"Okay."

"Would you ever need smaller private aircraft to transport survivors from the point of rescue to safe houses, medical facilities, or family reunions?"

I thought I heard the phone drop. After a gasp and a pause, I heard, "You have no idea what an answer to prayer that would be."

For the next twenty minutes, she explained several recent rescue stories where trafficking survivors were in serious danger because they lacked transportation out of their immediate environment. The survivors had decided to leave and get help, but could not reach another city or location quickly and efficiently. Usually, they had no ID, car, or money. Organizations like Trafficking Hope would drive survivors to their destinations, usually resulting in twelve-to-sixteen-hour road trips that were neither safe nor sustainable for the survivor or the rescue organization. On-demand air transportation was a missing piece of the rescue equation. I did not know this, but God did.

She went on to describe how several trafficking survivors were recently rescued by law enforcement, but at the end of the day, law enforcement – state, federal, and local – is not in the transportation business and cannot get trafficking survivors to safe houses in another state. It's just a reality. Being able to access private air transport would be a complete game changer, a blessing beyond compare, and would immediately save lives.

"Oh, good! I am not crazy."

"Well then, Ted, do you mind if I pray over you and this idea, because you will have an organization with a fleet of airplanes, and you will be rescuing many people."

That pleasant, eager, and now cheerful voice prayed over me and God's vision for me on that phone call. As she prayed, I felt the Holy Spirit pour into me. I had no idea how this would happen or when; all I knew at the end of that phone call was that it would happen, and God would do all of it because I could do none of it.

I was thrilled after that phone call; the seeds of God's vision were placed in my hand, and all I had to do was plant them, though I had no idea how. Furthermore, I had not the slightest idea about the scope or what creating an operation like this would entail. If I had known the slightest aspect of starting an enterprise of this magnitude, I would instantly have said, "This is impossible," and would never have gone down that path.

God knew this. That is why He gave it to me only in small pieces, as a progressive revelation. If He had given it to me all at once, it would have overwhelmed me and seemed impossible.

Anyone who has walked with Christ for a long time will tell you, "Expect some time in the dirt." Seeds are planted, then you water, and then you wait. No one is good at this. About nine months went by where it seemed like nothing was happening, but under the surface, God is always working. As long as you continue watering, the roots are always growing deeper. As I kept this in prayer, the vision of rescuing trafficking survivors grew stronger. I started doing more research on trafficking and trafficking-rescue organizations. I started calling other rescue organizations to talk about everything from their transportation needs to all their other needs. I had a million questions: How did they operate? What was their annual budget? How many employees did they have? What kind of insurance did they have, and most importantly, how did they get started?

All were receptive and had their own God-sized story to share, and every organization I reached out to was Christian-based. They all were. Very slowly it occurred to me that God was clearly in this fight on every front.

Over the next few months, I had a whole new group of acquaintances I had met just by cold-calling them, and all of them became like-minded friends. During this quiet time, I fielded a few phone calls from Trafficking Hope, where they needed to get a trafficking victim out of a horrible situation. One story in particular kept me up at night. They had called on a Tuesday afternoon, frantic. "Ted, can you help? We have a survivor who was beaten so badly that she has been in the hospital for several days. Her trafficker is literally waiting outside the hospital parking lot to pick her up and put her back into service. Can you get her out of here?"

She needed transport to a rescue facility in another state but had no way to get there, and nowhere to go. No friends or family could come to get her, and she had no one to call. Law enforcement could take her statement, but they couldn't keep her or take her anywhere.

I couldn't organize transportation that fast. I was paralyzed. There were more and more stories like this, trafficking victims left stranded. Law enforcement can only do so much, but they are not in the transportation business. Survivors cannot just get on an airplane; they have no identification and usually no money. For the most part, trafficking survivors have been off the grid for a while. The need for immediate transport is vital. God was about to ignite a series of events that would provide exactly what was needed.

On a Tuesday, sitting in a large government conference room in DC with about thirty people all staring at each other across a table in a meeting whose purpose I cannot recall, I suddenly felt the room go silent. It was the same silence I had heard that night in Annapolis, and the same silence I had heard that day on the airplane.

Stamped and imprinted on my mind, God whispered to me all the words at once: "Invisible Angels."

Then silence.

Then "InvisibleAngels.org. Buy the domain name Invisible Angels."

Like all the Bible characters we have read about, my first response was like theirs: "God, that domain is going to cost three thousand dollars."

"Buy the domain name now, please."

I got up from the table, walked around to my office, went

to www.register.com, opened my account, and entered "invisibleangels.org." "Available" popped up. "Available. $30." Stunned and a bit shaky, I immediately purchased the domain name, and as I clicked on the purchase button, God said two things: "Write a budget for this organization and speak life into this as if it's up and running."

From that exact moment, without a plan, business cards, a website, or even a bank account, all I did was talk about it as if Invisible Angels were flying around the country, recovering human trafficking survivors. I told everyone about a ministry that didn't yet exist, didn't have an airplane, and that the guy in charge really didn't have a clue, but God told me to keep speaking. Keep speaking life into Invisible Angels as if it were in full operation.

This is how God began to breathe life into this ministry, defying logic, speaking life into dry bones, creating streams in the desert. Now, God was preparing to open the floodgates of His provision and power.

The budget was another issue entirely. Over the next few months, my prayer time centered around the budget. "A budget for what?" I asked God.

"Invisible Angels. Write a budget for the ministry. Include everything: an airplane, aircraft expenses, everything you will need."

I am the guy who failed accounting twice in college, even with a tutor. And now God wants me to write a budget? "Clearly, Lord, You have the wrong guy."

"Write the budget."

So, over the next few months, I began putting together a budget for a ministry that didn't exist, had no volunteers, no bank account, and lacked one necessary component: an airplane. In truth, I had no idea what I needed, but God knew the exercise I needed to start effectively planning and preparing for what He was about to deliver, and He prepared me by shutting down the entire world . . . by COVID.

For the next year, while the world was shut down, the Word, the Holy Spirit, Jesus, and God our Father were on full throttle in my heart. I found myself in online Bible studies every night of the week: Mondays in an online group at Elevation Church in Charlotte; Tuesdays at National Community Church in Washington, DC; Wednesdays at Bayfront Church in Sarasota; Thursdays at Hope City Church in Texas; and Fridays at Radiant Church in Tampa. It was a year of free seminary.

Every morning, National Community Church in Washington, DC had an online Zoom call at 7:00 called Upper Zoom, a brief sermonette given to as many as five hundred people worldwide, sometimes more. The year flew by, and God had put me in an entirely new place with Him. No dating, no physical people in my life, really, for about a year. Just me, my Bible, and boxes.

Even though the whole world was shut down, the aviation community was still working. It couldn't have been a better time to work on my instrument and commercial ratings. It couldn't have gone better. Absolutely no distractions, and I completed both ratings consecutively. No interruptions and no problems. I completed my instrument rating in the fall of 2019 and my commercial rating in the spring of 2020. Done. I also flew about three hundred hours a year, which is a lot.

Still speaking life into Invisible Angels as if it were already up and running. I had the budget, which was several pages long by now, and since I loathe looking at Excel spreadsheets, I created more of a brochure. It looked nice, explained the mission, and was inviting to curious eyes; it turned out to be a road map for what was needed. Throughout the year, God continued to say, "Keep speaking life into it."

On my Wednesday night Zoom group at Bayfront Community Church in Sarasota, Florida, I told my new friend Robert, a recently retired United Airlines pilot, about the ministry's vision. He thought it was amazing.

"I know the perfect plane for you! You need a Cessna P210. It is perfect for this type of mission. It is a six-seater, but really it is designed for four people comfortably; it is pressurized, has plenty of power, can cruise at flight levels of up to twenty-five thousand feet, and it is economical to operate – about three hundred dollars an hour – and it's fast! Really fast!"

Getting online at www.trade-a-plane.com later that night, I looked at several Cessna P210s. Sure enough! It was the perfect plane for Invisible Angels. Everything Robert said was spot-on. Several were listed for sale online, ranging from $200,000 to $500,000. I thought about buying one, although I really couldn't afford an aircraft of that caliber, but I still considered it.

Although God had me isolated during this season, He was also weaving new relationships into my life. Dave, an FAA colleague I had met on a project earlier in 2020, happened to live about an hour south of me and would become incredibly instrumental to Invisible Angels in the upcoming year. My new pilot friend, Robert, who told me about the P210, had a daughter who happened to work at a human trafficking rescue organization called Selah Freedom. She introduced me to Laurie Swink, one of the co-founders and director of Selah Freedom. Laurie and I instantly hit it off. She recognized a God-driven vision when I walked through the door.

I drove down to meet Laurie and took a brief tour of their facility. About ten years old, Selah Freedom was well-funded and well-organized. And it was beautiful. It had multiple facilities in the central Florida area and was graduating twenty-five to thirty people a year from a two-year residential program focused on healing human trafficking survivors.

Laurie told me how it all started, just like Invisible Angels. God gave Laurie a vision fifteen years earlier, when she was a special-education teacher, and Selah Freedom started there. She knew exactly where I was coming from and where God was taking me.

We sat down, and I started sharing God's vision for Invisible Angels. She got it, every bit of it. We talked about how we could work together in the future and how badly they needed rescue transportation for survivors. We met for about an hour, and as I got up to leave, she mentioned that she had a huge work project that she had no idea where to even begin.

"What is it?"

"Well, I have to convert Selah Freedom's entire training program into an online training curriculum, within a learning management system, and create multiple eLearning courses. The board wants to create this and offer it to other rescue organizations as a new revenue source. You wouldn't know of anybody who does that, would you?"

I smiled. Only God. "I have been doing that for the past twenty-five years."

"You're kidding!"

God is always working. During the next few months, I had several meetings with Laurie and her team and got them pointed in the right direction. Within a few months, they had begun producing courseware within one of the industry's leading eLearning authoring platforms and learning management systems. They built the courses very quickly, and within the year, it became a revenue generator for Selah Freedom and provided valuable training for other rescue organizations across the country. Only God can do that.

Through Laurie and Selah Freedom, I met the directors of Life Recaptured, Created of Tampa, and other valuable contacts, which would all lead to future rescue transportation with Invisible Angels. Laurie and Selah Freedom became a key relationship for Invisible Angels.

Outside of the eLearning activity with Selah Freedom, another nine months of apparent inactivity passed for me and Invisible Angels. I met many new people, but it seemed like I was in a holding pattern. I did complain a bit during that time, which is really the reverse of prayer. I had heard and felt God's promise, but it looked like nothing was happening.

As I went about those nine months, God was growing and stretching me. He brought new people and new relationships into my life and removed old ones – new Christ-centered friendships and business relationships that blossomed before my eyes.

My five-nights-a-week Zoom groups continued, and my personal walk with Christ grew in ways I never thought possible. Of course, I couldn't see it as it was happening; we can't see trees grow either. I began to hear from God in a continuous stream, like a wireless network. The outside world grew silent, and the distractions in my life faded. It was just me, God, and my online Bible studies for nearly two years. It was amazing, and just when I thought things would stay silent for a while, God was about to bring the walls of Jericho down.

Nine months after my friend Robert told me about the perfect plane for Invisible Angels, I was in DC for a work trip. On a Sunday night, I was in my condo listening to Stephen Furtick deliver a sermon called "When God Gives You the Green Light."

This sermon spoke to me; it was on fire. Everything about it described this entire season of waiting, personal growth, hearing God, loss, fear, solitude, and the seasons of nothing. This sermon described my entire journey from the original vision of Invisible Angels several years earlier to that very night. It was heavy and carried a ton of weight, almost pregnant with expectation. I wanted to look for things that weren't there. I was walking around my tiny DC condo, almost expecting something; it was almost explosive, but I didn't know what it was. I just had this enormous, overwhelming sense of expectation.

A little while after the sermon ended, I went online to www.trade-a-plane.com just to look at planes. I don't know why, but I did. The very first airplane for sale that popped up was a Cessna P210. The ad simply said, "I want to donate this airplane to a nonprofit."

This was just as Robert had said nine months earlier, and it was in perfect condition. I sat frozen, my hands shaking and the oxygen leaving my lungs. I stared intensely to make sure I was really seeing this. I was staring at an answer to a prayer I hadn't even prayed yet. It wasn't disbelief; it stared right back at me. The only way I could describe it is that it stopped time for me. The exact plane Robert told me about was sitting there right in front of me, and somebody wanted to give it away.

There was no phone number, just an email reply. I collected myself, which only lasted for a second, until I imagined all the other people in the world who wanted that exact plane for their nonprofit. Then, I started to panic again. I stopped, composed myself, and wrote a brief email response. I can't remember exactly what I said, but I described Invisible Angels' vision, mission, and how the plane would be used. I hit *submit* and prayed.

By 11:00 the next morning, I had probably looked at the ad 17,211 times, give or take a few, to make sure it was still there. It was, and around 11:30, I got a call. "Hi Ted. I'm Bill Strong, the owner of the Cessna P210."

That phone call was a blur. I was probably speaking at Mach 2 and most likely didn't make any sense. After a few minutes on the phone, Bill probably got tired of listening to me and gently said, "Slow down, son. I want you to have the airplane."

Melting and exploding, I was filled with crazy energy and paralyzed by God's glory simultaneously. God had split the Red Sea right in front of me. Everything God had been doing up to that point instantly poured back through me like a liquid replay. Everything started to play back, from the season of nothing, to what God said to me on that first solo flight, to the vision He was laying out for Invisible Angels, to the prayerfully prophetic phone call with Trafficking Hope, to Robert telling me this would be the perfect plane – now a reality.

The actual gravity of receiving this blessing was the closest thing to Jesus actually entering the room. He didn't need to though. He had been there the entire time. Without a bank account, business cards, or even a website, Invisible Angels now had an airplane.

Now the work needed to begin. At this point, Invisible Angels was only a name and a vision. I needed to:

- Set up a business bank account,

- Set up a not-for-profit LLC,

- Create a website,

- Apply for 501(c)(3) designation through the IRS,

- Put together a board of directors,

- Create bylaws for the corporation,

- Set up a PayPal donor account and acquire donors, and

- Create a vision statement.

I already had the budget and people who already believed in the vision. That's really all I needed at this point. People are curious, "How do you know when it's God?" Many times, as least for me, this is how: when you have an unexplainable miracle right behind you and an insurmountable task directly in front of you. And when God gets you through it, it's incredible confirmation of His provision.

I created the above list sitting on the floor at my coffee table and just went at it step-by-step. I opened a business bank account with one hundred dollars, got on www.LegalZoom.com

and set up the nonprofit very easily, and got all my corporation documents delivered and filed. Within the week, Invisible Angels was a corporate reality with one hundred dollars in the bank. It was real!

Bill and I had arranged to meet the following week in Kansas City. I had all the corporate documents and a donation agreement with me. I flew out and was met by a friend of Bill's who took me to see the airplane. It was perfect; it was in fantastic condition, very well maintained, and had complete logbooks. The engine had recently been overhauled. It could not have been better. Bill's friend went through the maintenance manuals and logbooks with me, and everything was in perfect order. Now it was time to see Bill.

Bill was in a rehabilitation hospital. He had been there for quite some time due to losing the use of his legs. We chatted for a while, and I thanked him. We went over the donation agreement, made a few changes, and we both signed it. Invisible Angels now had an airplane.

We arranged for me to come back and pick up the plane and fly it back to Florida, but Bill had a friend fly it out. In late October 2021, Invisible Angels took possession of its first airplane.

Airplanes are not like cars. You don't just hop in and fly them away. Some aircraft require specialized-type ratings, and all aircraft require extensive training. When I told other pilots that Invisible Angels had acquired a P210, every single pilot said the same thing: "The P210 is a very complex aircraft. You need to treat that airplane like an airliner."

They were right. The P210 is a lot of airplane.

In aircraft ownership, you don't move the airplane unless you have insurance. Don't even start the engine or open the doors. In fact, don't even look at it! It stays in the hangar until it's insured. Airplanes are incredibly complex and expensive machines. The insurance companies want to protect their investment, and it is in their best interest to have safe, well-trained pilots, so insurance training is mandatory on almost every aircraft of this caliber. This was no different.

I did not have a lot of hours in what are called complex airplanes. The P210 is pressurized, turbocharged, has retractable gear, a very powerful engine, and a variable-pitch prop. The POH, or *Pilot's Operating Handbook* (the owner's manual), is the size of an old, thick library edition of *Webster's Dictionary,* and you have to know that manual inside and out. This is not a plane you just hop in and fly. You need extensive training.

By now, I had a little over eight hundred hours of flight time before I got into the P210. The insurance company wanted me to have twenty-four hours of training, specifically in the P210, before they would provide coverage. They provided a list of training facilities and private instructors. Choosing an instructor from the list, I made a phone call. A joyous voice answered.

Instantly hitting it off with Ron, who began his flying career with combat experience in Vietnam, he is the guy you want to teach you how to fly a complex aircraft. He sounded like he was about forty, looked about sixty-five, and I almost fell over when I found out he was eighty. Ron is a pilot's pilot. He is inspirational to be around, probably because of the twenty-thousand-plus hours of flight time he has accumulated in every type of flying machine imaginable. After two long days of training, Ron signed me off on the airplane.

Invisible Angels was officially a reality.

CHAPTER 7

FIRST RESCUE

"Very truly I tell you, whoever believes in me will do the works I have been doing, and they will do even greater things than these, because I am going to the Father. And I will do whatever you ask in my name, so that the Father may be glorified in the Son. You may ask me for anything in my name, and I will do it." (John 14:12-14 NIV)

Some may read this verse and on the surface, it may appear as a personal guarantee from God for a genie in a bottle: *"I will do whatever you ask in my name."* Anything we want, and it will be given. We forget, or most likely do not fully understand, the *"in my name"* part. The last thing Jesus is talking about here is a bottomless credit card for answered prayer. Rather, these verses are an invitation to alignment. John 14:12-14 is an invitation to align yourself with God's will and what He is currently doing in and through your life. When you stop and think about it, if you are aligned with God's will, He will give you whatever you need to accomplish it. That is who He is!

Up to this point, Invisible Angels was birthed by the sole lead of God's will and direction. It was hours past obvious, and anyone looking or listening in from the outside knew I couldn't take credit for any of it; I simply did not have the ability to make any of this happen. Everything that had happened and was delivered was the end of a chain of God-given miracles, and unmistakably God's will. From the cloud engulfing the airplane on my solo flight four years earlier, to our aircraft being donated, everything had just been revealed and delivered in God's perfect timing. John 14:12-14 was happening in real time for me, except there was one difference: God was delivering several steps ahead of me.

God was helping us in situations we hadn't even prayed for, most likely because I did not know what I needed. God was providing everything in His perfect order and perfect *kairos* timing. This cycle of miracles repeated itself in nine-month periods. Now, what else happens in nine-month periods? Birth. This lines up exactly with God's Word in Isaiah 66:9 (NIV): *"Do I bring to the moment of birth and not give delivery?" says the* LORD. *"Do I close up the womb when I bring to delivery?" says your God.* Certainly not. God delivers what He gives birth to.

Several weeks after the insurance training, a pilot friend volunteering with Invisible Angels strongly suggested forming a prayer team to pray for the entire ministry. I completely agreed. Every trip and survivor being transported absolutely needed to be prayed for. A completely spiritually protected path through the sky must be created for every flight and all related activities. To be protected, Invisible Angels needed to operate completely within and by the authority of John 14:12-14. The airplane, maintenance personnel, and even air traffic controllers needed prayers. Every aspect needed to be covered in prayer, no matter how minute.

A ministry going headfirst into this level of demonic spiritual battle would be utterly defenseless without a team of people pray-ing for each survivor and every flight. Without prayer, Invisible Angels would be vulnerable in every aspect. We began to talk about when we could all get together and meet, but before the first prayer meeting group could happen, I received a phone call from Selah Freedom needing transport for a survivor. This would be our first flight.

I hadn't thought much about how calls for rescue transpor-tation would come in and how they would be handled. I was just following God's lead, really chasing after God's lead at this point because I didn't know what to expect. I truly didn't know what I didn't know; from what I hear, this is a common theme for anyone involved in ministry.

The coordinator from Selah Freedom explained that a woman needed transport from her location to Selah Freedom in the Sarasota, Florida area, about five hundred miles away. She had been apprehended on drug and weapons charges. Unfortunately, this is an all-too-familiar scenario for traffick-ing survivors. They are usually arrested for, and along with, the crimes their traffickers commit: drugs, weapons, prostitution, trafficking, and everything else that *the life* entails. After she was taken into custody and questioned by detectives, Emma's full story began to emerge.

Emma's journey follows a similar storyline: getting wrapped up with the wrong people, thinking it won't happen to you, then add drugs, weapons, and prostitution, and trafficking isn't far behind. The entire environment and culture can swallow the survivor whole. Once that point is reached, from the survivor's perspective, it may seem impossible to get out.

Emma was one of several women held in a house by multiple traffickers. It was unclear how long they had been held; it may have been a few years. Leaving untethered did not end well. The traffickers caught up with them quickly, resulting in multiple homicides. Piecing the story together, detectives discovered Emma, along with several others, had been trafficked for quite some time. Kept in protective custody for several weeks, detectives completed their investigation, and social services and another rescue organization were brought in to find solutions. Selah Freedom was contacted to see if they could help. Selah Freedom had space available, but they needed to get her there.

Now Selah Freedom had a way to do just that. Organizing everything over the phone with Selah Freedom, a window of travel days was selected – weather permitting – and all necessary background information from the survivor was collected. Her weight and overall health were documented. Then, releases and MOUs were signed. We also needed to ensure she was comfortable traveling in a smaller aircraft and that she was not using or carrying any drugs or anything illegal. Being that she would be coming directly from jail, it was unlikely, but along with needed documentation, that was also about establishing a strong safety culture within Invisible Angels. For everyone's safety, no gaps could be overlooked.

Early on, during one of the nine-month miracle periods, it was decided that Invisible Angels must always travel with a survivor advocate from the safe house or rescue organization for which we were conducting the flight. The advocate is there to hold the victim's hand and guide them throughout the journey. Nicole, from Selah Freedom, was our advocate on this first trip.

This flight was relatively simple: ten minutes from our home airport to the pickup airport to get Nicole, then two hours north to pick up Emma, two hours back down to drop off Emma and Nicole, then ten minutes back to our home airport. Just before 8:00 that morning, landing at the pickup airport, I taxied toward the private terminal where the ramp agent directed me to park on the other side of a bright, shiny, $10-million Falcon jet. It was a celebrity beauty; something Taylor Swift might own. Well, it happened to be the same type of jet she owns, I found out later. But I thought nothing of it then, as I see these planes all the time and simply feel lucky when I get to park next to them.

After shutting down, I got out and walked past the parked jet and into the terminal to meet Nicole. Not having met before, we chatted for a minute, and I sat down to brief her about today's flights, what to expect regarding the weather and emergency procedures, and I answered a few of her questions. She seemed really excited as we were walking out to the airplane, a bit too excited. I couldn't figure out why until I looked straight ahead.

We were walking directly toward the shiny, glowing Taylor Swift private jet. Glancing slightly over at Nicole, she suddenly had a new strut in her walk with a huge smile on her face. I couldn't break it to her. In about six seconds, her dream for the day would be shattered. Executive-level, $10-million private-jet human trafficking recovery wouldn't be happening this morning. Maybe one day, but not today.

We headed for the front of the private jet, and Nicole's face was bursting with excitement. I started to feel bad as I kept walking past the nose of the beautiful private Falcon jet, and the excitement on Nicole's face melted as we turned around the nose of the Falcon, revealing the much smaller Invisible Angels aircraft, the little one with the propeller. It was dwarfed by the $10-million shadow of the highly insured aviation beauty. Clutching her coffee, Nicole muttered, "Well, this is much smaller than I expected."

I said to her, "One day, Nicole. Keep praying."

We got into the Invisible Angels aircraft, the one with the propeller, got our clearance, taxied toward the runway, and departed for the two-hour trip north. It was a beautifully smooth, uneventful trip until we were about thirty minutes from our destination. While en route, checking the satellite weather and talking with center controllers, the weather had taken a turn for the worse at our intended destination. A line of thunderstorms had suddenly developed, removing the option to land there.

Thunderstorms can develop rapidly and are no match for smaller aircraft. Larger private jets and turboprop aircraft can easily climb above and around the weather, but not us, not yet. Texting with the rescue organization, Nicole notified them that we had to divert due to weather and change airports about eighty-five miles short of our original destination. This may have been inconvenient, but passenger safety and comfort must come first.

Early on, I decided that Invisible Angels would not fly in bad or questionable weather. This single decision eliminated an enormous amount of risk. In fact, this transport request from Selah Freedom that we were flying today was not the first call I received from them. Just a couple of days after I completed the insurance training, I received a call from Selah Freedom for a much shorter trip, but a low-pressure system combined with a continuous line of thunderstorms completely covered the proposed flight path. It was forecast to remain that way for the next forty-eight hours. I declined the trip, telling them the weather would not clear for the next two days. It was only a 250-mile drive, and it would have been safer to transport her by car, which is exactly what they did. I was very happy to decline our first flight request because of my no-fly decision. You do not get a second chance to implement proper safety protocols in aviation. This decision also assured Selah Freedom that Invisible Angels would always prioritize safety. That is a reputation every aviation organization must strive for.

Landing at the new pickup location, we walked into the private terminal where we waited for Emma to arrive. We had a little more than ninety minutes. Whatever picture you have in your mind about what human trafficking survivors are like, it's just the opposite. They look just like you and me, just like your kids or their friends, just like your neighbor or their friends, and just like anybody else you have ever seen.

The difference is that these people have been sold for sex, on average, ten to twelve times a day, and usually for years. These are Americans, not foreigners or illegal immigrants. Survivors range from teens and twentysomethings from affluent communities, to children and preteens in the foster care system. More horrifying, a large percentage of trafficking survivors are sold by family members or lured into trafficking by people they know. They range from the very young, under ten years old, to suburban mothers in their forties. This is all happening, invisibly, right in front of us. They are just like anyone you have ever seen.

About ninety minutes after we landed, Emma came walking into the private terminal, escorted by the advocate from the recovery group that organized her release. Emma looked like any other woman in her early thirties. With a beaming smile, she told us she was a little nervous about flying because she had never been on a plane before. She had been in jail for several weeks, confined to the medical unit for her safety, so she was glad to be out. She was also very eager to leave. We spoke briefly with the advocate who organized her release and talked with Emma about the flight, explaining the necessary safety procedures and all other safety information passengers need to know.

Emma had just one question: "Will I see a beach?"

"Yes, we can make that happen for you."

In a few minutes, we were packed, on the airplane, and on our way. We were able to give Emma about an hour-long ride right down the coast, over some of the most beautiful uninhabited shoreline in the country. Nicole handled Emma with grace, warmth, and compassion. Emma obviously felt very comfortable with Nicole; both were so chatty that I had to switch their conversations off in my headset so I could concentrate on getting us back home.

The one thing that stuck with me is that Emma had dreams and goals. Overhearing their conversation, she wanted to become a veterinary technician – completely doable, and easy, as a matter of fact. She told Nicole about wanting to open a shelter for abused dogs. Once we were at cruising altitude, with the flip of a switch on the panel, I could pop in and out of their conversation. I really enjoyed listening to Emma tell Nicole about her dreams. She had a goal and a plan. That, and hard work, is all anyone needs to start and realize their dreams.

The ninety-minute ride went by fast, and just before sunset, we landed. I walked Nicole and Emma back into the private terminal where Nicole and I had met earlier that morning and I said my goodbyes. I got back into the Invisible Angels airplane for the ten-minute trip home, and Nicole took Emma to Selah Freedom's intake facility and safe house. Our first recovery trip was complete and, by all measures, a success. Invisible Angels provided safe, secure air transport. Emma had made it safely to Selah Freedom's intake facility and safe house, where she would have a secure, safe place for the next two years, with all the services and care she would need.

Flying the ten minutes back to our home airport, I realized what God had just done. This day was the culmination of a crescendo starting three years earlier. I could not have done any of this by myself. I am unqualified, underfunded; I wasn't even a pilot six years prior. I knew nothing about human trafficking, and I had no idea this was even needed. I can take credit for none of it. I was literally just along for the ride. If anything, I was just the driver. God had recovered someone from the horrors of the trafficking life and placed her in an incredible and beautiful facility with everything she would need: twenty-four seven medical access and psychological staff, clothes, food, and most importantly, a safe place where Emma could start rebuilding her life. Invisible Angels got her there.

Unfortunately for Emma, this would only last about thirty hours.

Around 20 percent of the time, trafficking survivors go back. We cannot fathom that decision or even begin to understand it. Trauma that is that severe splinters off into hundreds of unexplainable reactions, decisions, and emotions that we cannot comprehend. Sometimes, our normal is not normal for trafficking survivors, and the shock of being in a safe and secure environment may be too unpredictable and simply too much. A day and a half after Emma had been flown to Selah Freedom, I received a call from Nicole.

Emma walked right out the front door.

Selah Freedom could not hold her against her will. She was an adult who agreed to go to Selah Freedom and complete a two-year residential program. If that agreement becomes broken, it is reported to the authorities, a warrant is issued for her arrest, and all original charges are reinstated. Sadly, the cycle can repeat itself. It's heartbreaking.

Emma was never heard from again.

This revealed what Invisible Angels is up against. This is a spiritual battle against unspeakable evil and demonic forces; spiritual warfare on a level I've never seen before. Invisible Angels must be seriously prayed for and prepared for this fight. Emma's departure set the tone for the reality of the arena God had placed us in. Prayer was not only vital but also the most important mission of this ministry.

About a week after Emma left, in a small, modest living room, ten powerful prayer warriors showed up for our first Invisible Angels prayer meeting. Most of us attended the same church, and although I had seen almost everyone at church, I had never really met any of them before. There was a surreal spiritual expectation in that small living room, and, not having much experience with this, I knew something huge would happen.

This was my first real prayer meeting, in many ways. I didn't know what to expect. I had always been in small groups, hungry for God's Word, and completely active in church. I also played in Christian worship bands for over twenty years. I obviously had prayed, but to be truthful, I was far too ignorant of the power and authority available to us through prayer. A solid devotion and commitment to prayer was something I had overlooked for most of my Christian walk. Looking back, I don't know how I survived this long.

As soon as prayer began, I was blown away by their passion in communicating with God, expounding on God's Word, believing God's promises for us, and creating a spiritual path for this newly formed ministry, Invisible Angels. As soon as God's words and promises were uttered, we could sense spiritual authority engulfing the room, creating a foundation of peace, power, and spiritual authority for everyone involved in Invisible Angels. Everyone in the room felt a spiritual lock-in and commitment to this cause. I had never felt such prayer before.

Up until that point, prayer for Invisible Angels hadn't been on my mind nearly as much as it should have been. Understandably, to some degree, I was in a constant catch-up mode with what God had been doing: focusing on putting the organization together from the airplane side; setting up the corporate and legal structure; making sure we had the right releases and legal paperwork; finding the right people to be involved; selecting the right board members; finding a place to keep the airplane; ensuring the maintenance was up-to-date and the records were in proper order; organizing the logistics needed; putting together the structure for how our flights would be organized, documented, and completed; and most importantly for any aviation organization, ensuring that everything within Invisible Angels was centered around safety.

And then all of this had to be funded.

God had told me early on, "Don't worry about the money." At first, I didn't, because I didn't know any better. We were a newly formed and registered nonprofit LLC, and we were beginning to accept donations. Our nonprofit status would be applied for soon, resulting in a testament to one of our biggest miracles, which you will learn about later. The money began to come in, not a lot, but exactly what we needed. From the moment we received the airplane, expenses racked up fast, as airplanes are enormously expensive. Insurance, mandatory recurrent flight training, flight navigation software subscriptions, regular and intermittent maintenance, fuel, supplies, hangar fees, navigation database subscriptions, headphones, tires, and all the necessary accessories added up unbelievably quickly.

Well before our first flight, we had about $12,000 in expenses and hadn't even left the ground yet. From the beginning, all my new friends in the nonprofit space told me the same thing: "All you are going to be doing from this point forward is raising money." That was soon the truth and my brand-new nonprofit reality.

As I mentioned, I was focused on everything else and hadn't even thought about the spiritual battle we would face. I had no idea of the level of spiritual protection that would be needed. We never would have made it without this prayer group. Once again, God was a step ahead of everything. Within the prayer group, the level of spiritual detail and the heartfelt depth of the prayerful requests prayed that evening bored a hole so incredibly deep into me that it revealed what the Holy Spirit had been waiting for me to do for almost thirty years: simply call on Him.

Jeremiah 33:3 (NIV) makes it crystal clear: *"'Call to me and I will answer you and tell you great and unsearchable things you do not know.'"* This is an invitation to accept the spiritual authority and power given to me the night I accepted Christ so many years ago. As part of a new group, all-in and prayerfully committed to this new ministry, I accepted the Holy Spirit's simple invitation to improve my personal prayer life. As these prayers continued to drill deep into me, there was also an extraction, removing previously held thoughts, conceptions, and misconceptions about prayer while simultaneously allowing the Holy Spirit to work inside me for what He wanted to do.

I didn't think prayer like this was possible; I never thought I would become part of a prayer group like this one. In one night, in just under two hours, this new group of friends started to teach me how to pray in ways I never thought possible. God just started to reveal and unveil His Spirit within me, and all I had to do was let the Holy Spirit speak. I just had to get myself out of the way and let God remove me from the equation.

This opened up a whole new spiritual dimension of the authority and power of prayer available to me that I knew was there; I just had yet to experience it and didn't know how to access it. It was as if I had a switch on my instrument panel, and I didn't know what it was for until someone pointed out that that little switch turns your tiny 25-HP engine into a nuclear reactor, which had been there the entire time.

This is also when I started to receive the gift of tongues. I received Christ in the last century, in 1988, and got my start in a charismatic, Holy Spirit-filled church, so I should have known this back then. I always felt comfortable in a charismatic environment. My salvation night was an on-fire Holy Spirit event, and from the beginning of my walk, I often heard people speak in tongues. I just never understood it. I thought it was undeniably awesome, and I knew it was a gift from the Holy Spirit, but I never ventured into understanding the gift of tongues. I just always thought it was a gift that would either come to me from the beginning or never happen.

As I matured in my Christian walk, I thought I had never received the gift of tongues, and I left it at that. The truth is I never asked for it, until one day I did. At home one night, in a moment of prayer, I asked God for the gift of tongues. And that is all it took. It just started to flow. From that simple request, the gift of tongues began pouring into my life, and my prayer life changed dramatically.

I went from praying, "God, please protect us, bless our food, and God, please cover us with your net of safety," to speaking with power and authority within God's will and what God was currently doing in me and within Invisible Angels. It was during this season that my prayer life took on a whole new dimension, and I, as well as others around me, began to see more miracles result after times of intense prayer and intercession.

That evening, the prayer group prayed over every aspect of Invisible Angels: the airplane, planning, maintenance, fuel, food, and future trafficking survivors who would be on that aircraft. My focus and ability in running the organization, as well as my health and safety as a pilot, our legal and financial needs, future maintenance needs, and future personnel needs, were included. Nothing was left uncovered. I truly felt that alignment take place between our desires and God's will, and above all, I felt the Holy Spirit come in and surround everything with a tangible level of peace and spiritual authority over our mission.

We would need it for who we were going to rescue next.

CHAPTER 8

OPERATIONAL

*"All who rage against you will surely be ashamed
and disgraced; those who oppose you will be as
nothing and perish. Though you search for your
enemies, you will not find them. Those who wage
war against you will be as nothing at all. For I
am the LORD your God who takes hold of your
right hand and says to you, Do not fear; I will
help you."* (Isaiah 41:11-13 NIV)

Long before the crisis comes, God is already moving. When
He rescues His children, the right people are already in their
proper place, handpicked, prepared, and perfectly timed.

As if she were in a rush, an older but familiar-looking woman
quickly made her way up the stairs and onto the stage. Almost jog-
ging and moving with the energy that defied her mid-seventies age,
she enthusiastically grabbed the microphone and started speaking.

Beaming through a wide, friendly smile, she didn't wait for an
introduction. "I wasn't even supposed to be here today, and when
I looked out the window at the weather, I didn't want to leave

my office. I mean, look outside! It's cold, thirty-five degrees, and it's dark and rainy! But I needed to come out here this morning and personally thank each of you for coming to this conference today and for working so hard to stop this horrible, unspeakable evil that is devouring our children. To law enforcement, rescue organizations, the universities, and to everyone here today, I want to celebrate the work you are doing and stand in agreement with you that God's children are not for sale."

Bursting into applause, the room felt the full force of Governor Kay Ivey's passion to do everything she could in her current position to fight human trafficking. This short but strong welcome set the tone for the next two days.

An annual event held during the first week of February, the END IT conference in Montgomery, Alabama, brings together federal, state, and local law enforcement, as well as dozens of rescue organizations, safe houses, and smaller organizations like Invisible Angels to share, coordinate, and learn about everyone's efforts. This was our first time attending the conference, and on our initial registration call, I was asked what Invisible Angels does. After telling them, the conference organizers were so excited and supportive that they gave us a free presentation table where we could share with all conference attendees what Invisible Angels does. They knew how badly air transport for the recovery of trafficking survivors was needed, and they did everything they could to help us.

The conference had dozens of brilliant breakout sessions, given by everyone from trafficking survivors to law enforcement, to share the latest information. We made dozens of new contacts and new friends, including one government agency that would result in removing a child from an unspeakably horrible situation just a couple of months later.

Every person and organization we encountered was incredibly supportive. This conference was invaluable for expanding our network and making people aware of our existence. Most trafficking rescue organizations attend this two-day event, and it becomes a very tight community by the end. The latest statistics were horrifying, and the most alarming number that stuck with me was that 70 percent of victims are trafficked by family members. That is exactly what we encountered next.

Our network expanded quickly. A few weeks later, we received a call from someone who knew someone who had talked to someone else who met us at the END IT conference. Glori, from Heritage of Hope, was on the phone, explaining that she had a survivor who needed to be taken to a safe house on the other side of the country as soon as possible for her protection. Separating her from her trafficker would prove more difficult than usual.

Her trafficker was her mother.

Just as she entered her teens, her mother began to sell her own child for drugs and rent money. It grew worse from there. Her entire teenage years were spent being traded and sold to local gang members. This was her teenage normal. As a pre-teen, she led a seemingly normal life, attending school and even being involved in a church youth group. That is where she originally met Glori, from Heritage of Hope, about ten years earlier. Glori was a youth leader in the same church, and they knew each other quite well.

Getting the background story from Glori, the girl just disappeared from the youth group. She stopped going. She never came back. No one ever knew what had happened or why she stopped going. I am sure no one had ever thought that her own mother had begun selling her off as a sexual commodity. Hearing the complete story, the trafficking ended by the time she was eighteen, when the survivor, along with three other girls, tried to leave. Her traffickers quickly caught up with them and threw all four of them into the trunk of a car. They were driven for a couple of hours through the night only to have the trunk opened and all four girls thrown into a pond in the middle of a forest preserve. Three were executed. Our survivor managed to escape through the woods to a gas station where she called a friend. The friend came and got her, but it was clear that she would be put back into *the life*. A few days later, our survivor said a prayer that revealed the depths of her unspeakable desperation: "God, if You are not going to rescue me from this, please kill me."

Later that same day, our survivor was were arrested on drug charges. Sitting in jail, she was mad at God that she had been arrested; furious, in fact. God was supposed to rescue her, not arrest her. Then, in a moment of silence, she realized that being in jail was God's answer to her prayer. God did rescue her. She was safe, and God was about to show up in an enormous way that she or anybody else would have never expected. God always works ahead of our problems, planting seeds and preparing solutions.

She was placed in a detention facility, the same facility where Heritage of Hope had an outreach ministry. Guess who, nearly ten years later, worked for Heritage of Hope? Glori.

Walking through the detention facility, Glori immediately recognized our survivor. Hugs, smiles, and tears of relief ensued as she told Glori her whole story, from age fourteen to eighteen, where she went, why, and most importantly, who was involved. Within a few hours, Glori knew everything.

Glori and Heritage of Hope immediately got involved and were able to get her recognized as a human trafficking victim. This completely changed the status of her incarceration. Over the next few weeks, Heritage of Hope found a wonderful facility with a two-year residential program, completely on the other side of the country, where she could start rebuilding her life, out of reach from those who were supposed to protect her. A week later, a judge signed off on the program request, and she was released to Heritage of Hope and her new facility for the two-year residential program. There was even better news: on successfully completing the residential program, all charges would be dropped, and she would have a clean record – a fresh start.

Now, Heritage of Hope just had to get her there.

Glori had called Invisible Angels, and we told her the trip was certainly something we could do; in fact, we couldn't wait. We were really excited for this one. Over the phone and through emails, after signing the necessary agreements, MOUs, and legal releases, we began planning the flights and getting everything prepared for the trip. Coordinating with Heritage of Hope, we selected a range of dates that would work and began making last-minute arrangements. But those were just the logistics; we had to have prayer for the entire operation in order to be fully prepared.

A couple of days later, and a day before the trip, the prayer group met for just under two hours, and we all started diving deep into God's promises and feverishly called on Him for His coverage, deliverance, guidance, and protection.

Being part of the prayer team, we prayed for this flight, for me as the pilot, for the airplane, for the air traffic controllers, and for Glori and our survivor; it was something just short of miraculous. I felt the same tsunami of the Holy Spirit engulfing the room as we all erupted in tongues, interceding for every level of spiritual protection and authority available to us.

Leaving that night, I felt we were completely covered; there was a peace that fell over me that evening and on the entire trip. This peace gave me the mental margin, the thought space to start something God had put on my heart several months earlier. Now was the time for this to be implemented.

When trafficking survivors are recovered, they usually have nothing: no clothes, no belongings, no identification, and certainly no money. This reality opened up a whole new ministry within Invisible Angels. They have only themselves and what they are wearing. During one of the nine-month gaps between the first prophecy and the airplane's delivery, God placed a backpack ministry on my heart. A backpack ministry didn't make sense at first, but it gradually became clear. Wouldn't it be awesome if survivors were given a backpack at the point of recovery, with some new clothes, toiletries, a Bible, a journal, and other personalized items?

After this had percolated in my heart for a while, it simply burst forth one day. Sitting in my office, working on a safety program, I felt the Holy Spirit telling me to stop, get in my car, and go to the mall to start talking to stores about donating their returned or damaged items to Invisible Angels. I did just that. About thirty minutes later, I found myself going from store to store at one of the largest outlet malls in Tampa, telling store managers who I was, what Invisible Angels did, what we needed, and how much of a positive impact it would make. This was completely led by the Holy Spirit. I had no plan and absolutely no idea how this would turn out.

At the end of that first day, I left the mall with about forty pounds of brand-new donated items from Lucky Brand, only to be followed in the next few weeks by donations from Brooks Brothers, Tommy Hilfiger, and Nautica. Just about every month since then, all of these stores have donated brand-new returned items, providing new clothes for the backpacks we prepare as well as delivering and donating the rest to safe houses and rescue facilities throughout the Southeast.

A couple of women from the prayer team handled the backpack ministry. With the donated clothes and some purchased items, Invisible Angels obtained the survivor's size, and prayed regarding the rest. It was perfect. For this survivor, they assembled a backpack complete with a Bible, a journal, sweatpants, T-shirts, necessary items, and some toiletries. But the most important item was something I never considered. The two women wrote the survivor a card and a prophetic letter describing God's love, plan, and Jesus as healer, comforter, and rescuer. I have never read this letter, nor any others written; I only heard about each survivor reading the letter on the plane, usually with tears streaming down their faces. This survivor was no different.

You never know what kind of impact something like this will have or what God is going to do with it. Matthew 24:35 (NIV) lays out the permanence of God's Word: *"Heaven and earth will pass away, but my words will never pass away."* God's loving words last forever. This is such a powerful ministry within Invisible Angels. Giving survivors something they can call their own from the minute they get on the plane is monumental. Giving them God's Word and a place to write down their thoughts makes it permanent.

With everything prepared for a long travel day, we departed early in the morning for the ninety-minute trip to the airport to meet Glori and our survivor. As we walked into the private terminal, Glori and our survivor sat in the waiting area. A little nervous about the unknowns, our survivor was very much looking forward to the flight.

As we all sat down to go over the necessary safety briefings and answer any questions she might have, we gave her the backpack prepared by the prayer team, complete with new clothes (all in her size), a journal, a Bible, and the prophetic letter written to her. She had told us she had never been on a plane before and was excited about the trip.

She had a ton of positive energy and was absolutely fascinated with everything about the aircraft. She was bright, funny, very engaging, had a million questions, and wanted to know everything about the aircraft and the trip. How fast would we be going? How did we know where we were going? What were all the gauges in the cockpit, and what do they do? How high were we flying? How much fuel was being used? In a very joyful way, she wanted to know everything.

Truly enjoying the flight, she seemed to settle in after a while and began going through her backpack, flipping through her Bible and writing in her journal. Glori had told me after the flight that she had read her letter written by the prayer team several times and was moved. Then, about an hour into the flight, she drifted off to sleep.

Arriving at our destination, her home for the next two years, we were met by intake coordinators from her new safe house. Getting off the airplane, our survivor seemed happy, relieved, and eager to move on. We said our goodbyes as she got into a van and was taken to her new safe home. Being very tired and hungry, we found the nearest restaurant for a well-deserved celebratory dinner. This was flight number two, and we realized where we had come from and where God had taken us. From the prophetic call with Trafficking Hope four years earlier to now, Invisible Angels was operational.

This trip was flawless. A long day with no issues, perfect weather. All the logistics lined up seamlessly. The backpack had an immensely positive impact, and we could see and sense our survivor experiencing the results of prayer. My prayer life became even deeper. I had a new sense of peace and newfound spiritual strength and authority. My prayer life grew more dynamic, intercessory, aggressive, bold, and fearless. I started to get the sense that these became prayers that would cause the devil to flee, as everyone in Invisible Angels and I were standing in the rightful authority God had given us. God knew this was exactly what was needed.

Now our phone began to ring.

Over the next few months, Invisible Angels grew. We started to feel the growth, becoming a real operational aviation ministry as we entered the early stages of organizational development:

forming, storming, norming, and performing. Some left the organization, and new people joined. We were just entering the forming stage, developing our policies and procedures, and narrowing our mission and vision statements. From the beginning, we didn't want to limit Invisible Angels to only providing recovery flights for survivors; we wanted to provide related air-transportation services as well – flights for family reunification, flights for lawyers defending trafficking survivors – really any related transportation that may be needed. One week, we received a call, again from Selah Freedom, except this time it was from the director and cofounder, and brand-new close friend, Laurie Swink, asking if we could fly a survivor to an event this coming weekend. Immediately I said yes without even asking what it was for, because I instantly knew it was exactly the type of flight and service we wanted to provide.

Holly Harris, a graduate of Selah Freedom's residential program, recently authored a book called *Relentless Survivor,* available on Amazon and an absolute must-read. Holly was asked to speak at an event in Merritt Island, Florida, a three-hour drive from the Sarasota area. Laurie asked if Invisible Angels could fly her there, saving both Holly and Laurie from a long six-hour drive for a forty-five-minute speaking event. Being a quick thirty-minute flight and a fun way to spend the day, and also celebrating the success of a survivor turned brand-new author, we enthusiastically agreed. After a quick flight, a car picked us up at the airport. We were whisked away to the event, where Holly did an amazing job as a newly minted keynote speaker, and all three of us had a wonderful lunch. About ninety minutes after we arrived, we were delivered back to the airport for the quick flight home. This was just fun.

Being there to aid and celebrate Holly's success is exactly the mission we want to provide to survivors on both sides of the recovery equation: quick, seamless air transport for whatever they may need and to wherever they may need to go. After the flight, I told Holly, "Anywhere in Florida you need to go to speak about your book, Invisible Angels will fly you there for free."

The miracles did not cease during this time, and the biggest miracle so far was moving all thirty-four hundred pounds of our empty aircraft into and out of the hangar. Two men, approaching sixty, accomplished this. Imagine pushing a small RV into and out of your garage by hand; that gives you an idea of what we faced every time we had to use the aircraft.

We desperately needed a motorized aircraft tug. There are ultra-advanced airplane tugs operated from an iPhone, connecting via Bluetooth, sliding under the nosewheel of the aircraft and locking into place, allowing you to move your six-passenger aircraft with your iPhone. Very cool and very expensive. Alternatives ranged from golf carts to modified riding lawn mowers until one of our volunteers, looking through airplane parts ads in the back of a local magazine, found a practical but very nice airplane tug for sale at $6,000.

Our volunteer called the number on a whim and said, "Hey, would you want to donate the tug to Invisible Angels?" He told him what we do, and in under thirty seconds, he said, "Absolutely." We picked up the tug the next day. We were astounded, but we shouldn't have been. God was still providing miracles for us, and He was nowhere near finished. He was about to reunite a mother with her child and put an entire US government agency, the Internal Revenue Service, into hyperdrive for a small aviation ministry on a God-sized mission.

From the flights we were making throughout the year, Invisible Angels became known to Homeland Security. With the initial phone call, we were reminded about the familial trafficking statistics from the END IT conference. Urgently, the agent jumped into the situation at hand. "We have an eight-year-old who has been recently rescued from a child pornography ring.

We need to get the child back to the mother. Can you pick up his mother, then fly up to meet our agent who has the child, and bring them both back home?"

Within a few hours, we were able to organize all the internal paperwork, flight plans, and check the weather for both legs of the trip. God brought the planning for this flight to a close in under three hours. Even the backpack was packed, and the prayer team went into action. Everything was covered. Calling the Homeland Security agent back was a thrill.

"Yes. We can do it. Tomorrow."

Homeland Security placed agents at both the departure and destination points. The mother was with us upon arrival, so a judge's approval for transporting a minor across state lines was unnecessary. Another agent was present at our destination to ensure our safe return home.

At 8:00 the next morning, after a short flight to pick up the mother, Invisible Angels was on its way to meet the agent waiting with the child. We didn't know how long he had been there, but that really didn't matter now. Getting both of them home safely, quickly, and quietly was the only thing that mattered.

By early afternoon, the mother and child landed safely and were in their own car driving home. Everything went perfectly. Homeland Security was thrilled. Sadly, the child's father and teacher had abducted the young child into a child pornography ring. That is all we knew. We took some comfort in being told, "The father and teacher will never see the light of day again." My blood boils when I hear about such cases, which are, unfortunately, many. People ask, "Doesn't this depress you? Aren't you sickened by this?" The simple answer is no, because we are doing something about it.

God implanted this ministry in my heart, so when we do these flights, it is joyful because we are a small link in the chain of actually stopping it. That brings about 30 percent of the mental peace needed. The other 70 percent comes from Matthew 18:6-7 (NIV): *"If anyone causes one of these little ones—those who believe in me—to stumble, it would be better for them to have a large millstone hung around their neck and to be drowned in the depths of the sea. Woe to the world because of the things that cause people to stumble! Such things must come, but woe to the person through whom they come!"*

There is no doubt that this heinous behavior was occurring during biblical times. Our species' depravity was sealed in the garden and is nothing new. I can close my eyes and imagine Jesus screaming this verse at the top of His lungs to the Pharisees and onlookers in the crowd, His voice quaking with rage, spit flying from His words and flicking off His beard, veins in His forehead bulging, tendons in His neck popping out with every inflection as He turned His head, yelling this into the crowd. As tempting as it is to want to take action, even in our thought life, we are ill-equipped and fall short mentally, spiritually, and physically. We don't have the eternal mindset and framework that God works in, outside of time. Vengeance is God's arena, God's problem, and God's responsibility. We're not made for that.

There is peace in Romans 12:19 (NIV): *Do not take revenge, my dear friends, but leave room for God's wrath, for it is written: "It is mine to avenge; I will repay," says the Lord.* There is peace as well in Deuteronomy 32:35 (NIV): *"It is mine to avenge; I will repay. In due time their foot will slip; their day of disaster is near and their doom rushes upon them."*

Eternity is a long time. Those who are guilty will have Jesus to deal with.

As we grew, we conducted more trafficking-related flights and recovery flights. We transported people from rescue organizations to necessary meetings, saving considerable time and increasing convenience. We also transported the directors of Selah Freedom to a fancy reception at the governor's mansion in Florida, to which we were invited. Our network of rescue organizations and safe houses grew rapidly. People learned about us, mainly because we were one of three organizations nationwide providing rescue and recovery transportation for trafficking survivors, and we were the only one with our own aircraft.

Life Recaptured in Merritt Island, Florida, contacted us to get a survivor from the other side of the country to their program. Not only a victim of human trafficking, she was also labor trafficked after taking refuge in a homeless shelter. Held in a three-bedroom apartment with up to twelve other women, their IDs and other personal items were taken from them upon arrival at a *promised job* program. They were forced to sign over their paychecks before they were even paid; they were told to *cover* expenses, and the situation grew worse from there.

We arrived in Merritt Island on a hot Florida afternoon, and as the survivor got off the aircraft, she came up to me, looked at me with eyes filled with gratitude, and handed me several papers. She had been writing down her story on the flight, and as she handed the papers over to me, she said, "Look, you have to understand something. Three years ago, I was a normal suburban housewife with three kids. It's all right here."

It was all there. Brief, but all there. I read in disbelief and turned everything over to an agent with Homeland Security and a friend at the FBI. You would expect this to happen in Eastern Europe in the 1840s, but not in America in 2022. The gravity and reality of the trafficking scenario in the United States were becoming louder and seemed to be getting worse, except that what was already happening was just being uncovered.

As we grew, we also received donations that funded the entire operation. God provided exactly what we needed, when we needed it, performing financial miracles at every step. He was about to show how serious He was about this fight by having an entire government agency act with lightning speed.

We needed to get our 501(c)(3) status approved. Anyone who has ever done this knows it is quite a simple online process, but absolutely necessary because the IRS must approve your mission. We never thought this would be an issue, and ever since the airplane's delivery, my faith expected miracles to happen, and they did because they were about to become huge.

The nonprofit approval status usually takes six months to a year. On Wednesday evening, a volunteer and I completed the online application at www.IRS.gov, entered our $750 in the credit card field, and submitted it. A pop-up IRS.gov window appeared, indicating we would hear from them within six months. That was Wednesday evening. The following Friday, ten days later, I had to be back in Washington, DC for meetings the next week. Arriving at my DC house on Friday night, I opened my mailbox to find the usual three to four weeks' worth of junk mail. Walking into my house, I dropped my bags in the hallway and went straight to the trash can to go through the mail. Still wearing my coat, I flipped through the mail, sliding the junk mail into the trash can. A letter from the IRS addressed to Invisible Angels appeared next.

When anyone receives an unsolicited letter from the IRS, it is rarely good news. I didn't even think it could have anything to do with our nonprofit status, since we just filed the application ten days earlier – really eight days if you exclude the weekend. There was no way it was related to our application; they don't move that fast. They can't move that fast; they are the IRS!

I opened the letter and, staring at the first line, I fell onto the couch. "Dear applicant, we are pleased to inform you that your nonprofit status has been approved." The IRS nonprofit 501(c)(3) approval for Invisible Angels was in my mailbox within ten days of hitting *submit*. God is the only one who can make the IRS move that fast.

Invisible Angels was now an operational, for-real nonprofit.

CHAPTER 9

SHUT DOWN

"As the heavens are higher than the earth, so are my ways higher than your ways and my thoughts than your thoughts." (Isaiah 55:9 NIV)

Sometimes life shatters overnight. One minute, everything's smooth. The next minute, it's spiraling fast. And in that chaos, we whisper, "God is in control," even as our hearts scream, "Is He?" We all know events can suddenly take a hard turn, ending up in a wreck, and we ask, "Why?" Everyone loves to quote Job when things suddenly blow up, but looking at this season from the finish line, Isaiah 55:9 describes more of God's plan during this season, more of what He was up to.

God had such an obvious reason for doing what He was about to do. He knew the trial coming up would be incredibly difficult for me, for those involved in Invisible Angels, and for friends who came to the rescue. For those looking at us from the outside, God was about to put us through a refining fire that would turn me inside out in a multitude of ways – personally, spiritually, and physically – as well as turn the organization inside out, allowing everyone watching to see the miraculous wonders God was about to do.

Except the last thing it felt or even looked like was a miracle.

Since the beginning, I had been telling of, and people could easily see, the miracles God had been doing over the last few years. The story itself became a huge testimony. Work friends and colleagues would call and ask about Invisible Angels. I had one friend call me up, and in the middle of our conversation, she stopped and said, "Every time I talk to you, I start to believe in God."

"Absolutely! That's because God is in this fight!"

The testimony of what God was doing was telling itself; all I had to do was show up and answer the call. Watching God work like this, from the inside out, was absolutely magnificent. Just over a year old, the Invisible Angels' story was an incredible testimony. I kept hearing three words loud and clear from God: "Tell My story."

Everyone saw Christ in the middle of Invisible Angels, and I was not shy about sharing. The office of communications reached out to me and asked if they could do a feature story on us. This would be shared with the entire FAA workforce, about fifty thousand employees worldwide. I thought this was a wonderful idea.

The article was released, and Invisible Angels got a little notoriety within a federal agency. Certainly, I thought this would yield a positive result. Maybe more donations? Growth? Maybe a federal agency would get behind us? Maybe another plane would be donated? In Matthew 19:26 (NIV), it says, *Jesus looked at them and said, "With man this is impossible, but with God all things are possible."* All things are possible with Christ. Turns out, *all things* means all things, including the bad or even the worst.

About a week after the article was released, I got a call from the Washington, DC Flight Services Directorate Office, or what is known as the FSDO. Nobody in aviation, from a pilot to a food-service worker, wants a call from this office. Maybe they were calling to congratulate me, ask how they could help, or just give me a pat on the back for the work we were doing. I can dream. It was just the opposite; it was the worst possible scenario imaginable.

In a very serious tone, an aviation safety inspector said on the phone, "Mr. Greenfield, we have received multiple comments and complaints about your recently released article. Let me be clear: you are flying passengers solely to transport them from one point to another, correct?"

This was a very carefully worded legal question, and instantly, I knew this wouldn't be a congratulatory call. This was a response practically right out of the Federal Aviation Regulations (FARs). In an instant, I knew this wasn't going to end well. Someone, or many people, complained to the Flight Service Directorate Office in Washington, DC, that Invisible Angels was operating an illegal air-charter operation.

I went on to explain. "Yes, we are providing rescue transportation for human trafficking survivors." Hoping he would say, "Oh yes, that's awesome! Please continue your wonderful work, and I'm sorry for the phone call!" I am a dreamer. He didn't say anything close to that.

"Yes, I saw that, which is admirable, but under what regulations are you operating?"

"We are operating under FAR Part 91, humanitarian charitable flights." In my heart of hearts, I truly thought these flights would be operating under FAR Part 91 charitable flights. I was wrong.

"Well, Mr. Greenfield, is Invisible Angels paying for the fuel and the overall operation of the aircraft?"

"Yes."

"Does Invisible Angels own the aircraft?"

"Yes."

"Mr. Greenfield, if your operation is advertising, or *holding out* [FAA-FARspeak for advertising] that Invisible Angels is in the business of providing air transport for passengers, Invisible Angels needs to be a Part 135 direct air-carrier operation. You may be operating in violation of federal law. We are going to open a compliance action against you. You will be notified by mail and receive a hearing date."

"Thank you."

The call ended.

This five-minute phone call resulted in Invisible Angels being shut down pending further FAA investigation. Just like Moses being trapped in the sand, Invisible Angels faced absolute impossibilities on all sides, and I now faced an FAA compliance action.

Compliance actions are very serious and are the worst thing that could happen. The results of a compliance action can suspend or revoke your pilot's license, impound the airplane, and, if found to be operating an illegal air-charter operation, the fines could be in the millions of dollars. To make matters worse, and even outright embarrassing, I was an FAA employee.

In the space of a five-minute phone call, I went from being on top of the world, watching God fulfilling His plan, doing exactly what God had called me to do, seeing continuous answers to prayer, completing multiple rescues, saving lives, and seeing God perform Red Sea-sized miracles for everyone to see, to only have it all come crashing down.

Stunned, I left my office, went to my living room, and sat on the couch. I was just trying to process the call. Then, over the wave of internal confusion, I heard God quietly say, "Don't worry. It will all be okay. Just tell My story."

At that moment, an incredible peace came over me. I

practically forgot about the phone call, as if it were a distant memory. I just continued my day, almost as if the call had never happened. I was covered in peace, an unexplainable peace. Philippians 4:7 (NIV) was in motion: *And the peace of God, which transcends all understanding, will guard your hearts and your minds in Christ Jesus.* The peace that truly transcends all understanding had come over me.

If God said, "Don't worry," I'm not going to worry. If I needed a reminder, all I had to do was drive to the airport, go into the hangar, and look at the donated $250,000 Invisible Angels airplane we owned. If that didn't work, I would just remember the rescues and write down every miracle God had provided up to this point. God didn't bring me here to leave me here, and God's plans do not fail. Whatever happened from that point forward would be an amazing testimony. I just had to walk through it. I was along for the ride, and all I had to do was be still, be obedient, stay focused on His Word, and remain continuously in prayer.

If only it were that easy.

To fully explain what we faced, I need to explain the Federal Aviation Regulations. They are extremely complex. Legally, the FARs are brilliant, but they could be viewed as unnecessarily restrictive and prohibitive from the public's or a private pilot's viewpoint.

The Federal Aviation Administration does not want pilots to fly for financial motivation unless they are commercially rated and have appropriate safety oversight. Different levels of safety standards exist with different ratings and air-carrier certifications, and the Federal Aviation Regulations save countless lives by being written precisely as they are. Primarily, FARs Parts 119 and 135 protect the transportation of passengers.

The FAA does not want air operators (pilots) flying passengers for financial or humanitarian reasons without proper safety oversight. This safety oversight is why the United States has the safest national airspace system in the world. The FAA rightly wanted that safety oversight to apply to Invisible Angels.

Becoming a direct air carrier would introduce new safety compliance standards to Invisible Angels' operation: mandatory aircraft inspections annually, and every one hundred hours of operation and random inspections. Annual pilot check rides with an FAA Operations Inspector, random drug testing for Invisible Angels' pilots, maintenance operators, and crew, as well as complete documentation of all aircraft and navigation system maintenance.

Becoming an FAA-sanctioned Part 135 air carrier would be a wonderful achievement for Invisible Angels and would immensely increase our safety standards. In fact, it would be the best possible scenario, allowing us to obtain sanctioned government contracts with state, federal, and local law enforcement, and other government agencies such as TSA (Transportation Security Administration), Homeland Security, CBP (Customs and Border Protection), FBI, and even the military; if allowed, we could even operate overseas. It would give Invisible Angels enormous legitimacy and the same rights and authority as any other chartered air-carrier operator. It would be huge, except that becoming a Part 135 air carrier is nearly impossible.

The reality of this happening was insurmountable. The Part 135 process takes about four years to complete, costs hundreds of thousands of dollars, and requires practically a full-time legal staff to create the necessary documentation. It takes an entire team from the FAA to create and approve the documentation, perform the pilots' check rides, inspect the aircraft multiple times per year, review and inspect all maintenance records and avionics upgrades, approve all documentation, and create the hundreds of necessary safety compliance standards.

Furthermore, the FAA practically has to invite you to apply to become a Part 135 air carrier. In many cases, becoming president of the United States is easier than becoming a Part 135 air-carrier operator. But then let's look at what God has to say about impossible things in Matthew 19:26 (NIV): *"Jesus looked at them and said, 'With man this is impossible, but with God all things are possible.'"*

I sat bewildered. "God, where do I go from here?"

"Just go."

"How?"

"Just go. Keep moving."

So I got up off the couch and made myself lunch.

Sometimes food can fix everything. I made a beautiful piece of salmon with vegetables, a salad, and some really good raspberry iced tea. In twenty minutes, I was back on the couch eating my lunch, watching the news with the sound off, when the phone rang. The person on the other end would be responsible for taking Invisible Angels and me through this next season of miracles. He transformed me from a private pilot with a commercial rating into a seriously safety-minded, forward-thinking commercial air operator. He had no idea how monumental his role would be in realizing God's vision and plan for Invisible Angels. He simply had no idea, but God did.

Dave is a work colleague I met on a project two years earlier. He lives about an hour away, and we got together socially several times. A bighearted believer, Dave organized the Bible study where our mutual friend Robert spoke the prophecy for the exact airplane we now own. Dave is an experienced airline pilot, former chief flight instructor for an airline, former corporate pilot, former aviation safety inspector, and he worked with the FAA Safety Team, creating educational programming and courseware for general aviation pilots. Dave had about forty years of aviation experience at all levels and was probably the best networker I have ever known. Dave knew everyone, and everyone knew Dave.

Dave called to say hi and see what I was doing over the weekend. I started chatting with him and casually mentioned that a compliance action had just been opened against me about an hour earlier for operating an illegal air charter.

Sounding as if he was practically losing his mind, Dave started screaming into the phone. "What? Do you know how serious this is? Who called you? When? Was it the Washington, DC FSDO? What was his name? Do you have a lawyer? You need to call Ed right away! How can you be so nonchalant about this? This is a huge deal! They can take your pilot's certificate, they can take the plane, they can fine you! This is enormous! How are you not freaking out?"

"God told me not to worry."

"Jesus would be freaked out if this happened to Him." (Dave actually said that.)

"I don't know; God just told me not to worry about anything. I don't know why I am not freaked out; I guess I should be. After getting off the phone, I heard God tell me, 'Don't worry. It will all be okay.'"

"You need to call Ed right away; in fact, hang on, I am getting Ed on the phone right now!"

Dave was completely losing it, which actually made me even calmer because I was thoroughly amused by the sound of him freaking out. It was hysterical. Also, it helps when someone is freaking out for you. Dave placed me on hold while he merged the calls.

Now, remember how God solves our problems upstream? Watch how God had already set this up about a year earlier.

Ed was a mutual friend Dave had introduced me to a year or so ago. Along with being an attorney, Ed was also a pilot and flight instructor. He and I had gone flying several times before, and I even made an awesome video for him of his seaplane. He has a popular, cool, and highly sought-after amphibious aircraft, a Lake Renegade, which is fun to fly. We went up, splashed down in several lakes across central-western Florida, and had an absolute blast. I knew Ed was a lawyer, but I had no idea Ed was Edward J. Page, a partner at Carlton Fields, PA, and probably one of Florida's, if not the country's, premier aviation attorneys.

Ed got on the line. After listening to Dave explain the situation, Ed said, "Uh-oh, Ted, you're in trouble."

"Yeah, I guess so."

Dave was still losing it as he quickly talked Ed into representing me at the compliance interview. Dave had this wrapped up before I realized who my friend Ed actually was. I had no idea that my friend, whom I went flying with a year earlier, would be the one to represent me before the FAA.

"Ted, can you and I meet this afternoon to review the case?"

"Yes."

Ed sent a Zoom link and told me to meet him online at 5:00 that afternoon, and then hung up. I was just putting things together and realized that in under two minutes, I now had the best legal representation possible. I hadn't done anything except answer the phone fifteen minutes earlier, and now I had Edward J. Page as my attorney. Dave was still beside himself as he sent text after text to me throughout the afternoon and was absolutely baffled that I was calm. I was baffled, too. The truth is, I had God's promise of peace, and keeping that peace was made much easier because watching Dave become unglued was just amusing. Again, Dave was freaking out for me.

Dave got me started filling out the necessary reports I needed to complete online, and over the rest of the afternoon, the gravity of the FAA's compliance action slowly started to sink in. I still had God's peace, but I realized how involved this process would be. Compliance actions can take years to resolve.

The paperwork that had to be prepared was significant.

Every flight that Invisible Angels took had to be documented, with an explanation of the flight's purpose, passengers, arriving and departing airports, flight path, weather, fuel receipts, flight plans, and everything else. This included every flight Invisible Angels took, from wheels up to wheels down, including fuel stops. There were over thirty flights.

I met with Ed later that day, and the gravity of the situation finally sank in. Again, I had the same peace of God over this entire situation, and I wasn't worried; I knew God would handle it, but I didn't know how to get through it. Ed started explaining compliance actions, and then said, "Ted, let's start at the beginning. Tell me how Invisible Angels got started."

A smile came over my face. Through a smile, I leaned into the laptop camera and said, "Ed, do you believe in God?"

As if Ed were on the witness stand in an episode of *Law and Order,* with ADA Barba staring right at him, the longest and most carefully considered one-word answer was released: "Yeeeeeeeeeessssssss."

Right there, during that long, one-word answer, I started to see what God was doing. This was where God was going to tell His story. I was just in the hot seat, along for the ride. It would truly be all okay. I still did not know how I would get through it, and I had no idea what the end result would be; all I knew was that God would perform another miracle and tell His story in the process.

I told Ed the entire story: from the initial vision in a Bible study and the call with Trafficking Hope, to meeting other rescue directors, the $30 domain, the budget writing, the airplane prophecy and donation, the incoming donations, the completed Invisible Angels rescues, and God's upstream placement at the FAA before any of it began. I probably spoke for thirty minutes, and then I stopped. Ed was taking it all in.

If I have learned one thing about giving testimony for Christ, it is this: Give the testimony, then get out of the way. Let God take it from there. From that point, it is between the person, the Holy Spirit, and God. Once the words leave your mouth, your job is done. I knew it sank in with Ed, and the sinking would continue during this entire process.

Ed prepared me for the upcoming interview, which was quite a lot of work. There was also another issue that I didn't know how I would get through. *How am I going to pay for this?* Ed told me his firm's rate was $895 an hour. I had $5,000 in my checking account.

"That's awesome, Ed. Can you get this done in about five hours?

Through a smile, Ed said, "Don't worry, we can work this out later. Let me talk to my firm and see if they can do this pro bono because of the work you are doing."

I knew God would handle this.

Ed and I met several times to go over my testimony, the facts, and the law – and within those meetings, Ed taught me one life-changing lesson I wish I had known forty years earlier. We are wonderfully and fearfully created in God's image. God knit us together in our mother's womb as a perfect creation of Christ. That being said, there is always room for improvement and areas to refine the incredible gifts God has given us.

I am high-strung and have an incredible amount of creative energy. I can always come up with a super, out-of-the-box, creative solution, and I am an eternal optimist. I speak fast, walk fast, work fast, get things done quickly, and usually see the shortest path to the finish line. All of those attributes are great, and it is how God created me, but the FAA does not want to see a bundle of "Jesus-crazy" energy on the witness stand. They will need to see a calm, safety-focused, forward-thinking pilot who made an honest regulatory mistake while keeping safety regulations at the forefront of his decisions.

Ed coached me and gave me one valuable piece of advice to get through this interview: "Ted, you need to learn to speak slowly. People will listen to you more carefully when you speak slowly, as if you have a Southern accent. Speaking slowly will give your words time to sink in."

For the interview with the FAA, I needed to provide and submit documentation for each Invisible Angels' rescue flight completed. Ed coached me on emphasizing the urgency of each flight, which was an actuality. These were individuals who escaped, attempted to escape, or were rescued from horrific circumstances. Several trips were rescue flights from situations resulting in homicides, including a young child forced into a child pornography ring. Human trafficking is real, it is happening, and this type of humanitarian mission is needed.

My interview day arrived. Several FAA safety inspectors were on the Zoom call, including the principal safety inspector who initiated the compliance action, along with Ed, and me. The tone was serious but pleasant, and the Zoom format seemed somewhat informal, which lessened the tension. Everyone worked from home, so they did not appear as intimidating aviation officials in a government interview room. They were all in their home offices, which was reassuring. It was a pleasant discussion of the facts and events leading to the compliance action.

The interview opened up, and one of the first questions the FAA safety inspector asked me was: "Ted, tell us how Invisible Angels began."

God had this, and I had some practice answering this one.

In a slightly forced drawl, I explained how Invisible Angels started, how it is a Christ-driven, Christ-centered ministry, and how we arrived at this interview. I told them of all the miracles that led to the birth of Invisible Angels. We then went into each flight, discussed the safety protocols, flight details, passenger information, and all other relevant information they needed. The Zoom interview was actually very pleasant.

One thing became clear: they all saw how God started Invisible Angels, what He provided, and how He provided it, and they were all deeply alarmed about the need for human trafficking rescue transportation. Like myself a few years earlier, they had heard about the trafficking problem in the US, but knew nothing about it. They had never been this close to it before, and now they had firsthand witness accounts. The safety inspectors were shocked to hear the individual accounts of each survivor we transported. I noticed the look on their faces as their knowledge of human trafficking quickly transformed from the training module that all FAA employees must take every year to hearing firsthand accounts of what is actually happening. As I looked at them over Zoom, I thought they all now had a chance to become part of the solution.

By the end of the interview, it was clear they all understood the urgency needed for rescue transportation, and I got the feeling they were there to help me. Even though I am an eternal optimist, I knew this could go either way. I was cautiously optimistic. This is the government, after all, and I worked there. I knew the culture and how some departments think. Would they just go by the guidelines and the rule book and then throw it at me? Or would they actually try to become part of the solution to this problem?

The call ended, and Ed said, "Now we wait."

Compliance actions can take months, even years, to close out, and Invisible Angels was shut down until we heard back from the FAA. I was prepared for a long wait. Psalm 46:10 (NIV) is the guide here: *"Be still, and know that I am God; I will be exalted among the nations, I will be exalted in the earth."* Just be still. The season of waiting will also bring the result of the season of planting.

Nothing fast happens at the FAA. It takes months to get safety programs approved, years for aircraft certifications or major changes to be made at an airport. Everything is reviewed, peer-reviewed, and reviewed again. Nothing happens fast there. This is because of a very solid safety culture embedded in everything they do, and although cumbersome, it is necessary.

Three weeks later, I received an email: "Mr. Greenfield, we have made a determination regarding your compliance action. Would you be able to meet online tomorrow at 11:00 a.m.?"

Forwarding the message to Ed, I wondered if he thought a fast jury return might not be good for the defense. I knew this could go either way, but I wasn't worried; in fact, I was just looking forward to the meeting to see what they had come up with. I still had the same peace I had when I received their original call. I knew God had already handled this situation; I just had to get His answer in His timing.

Ed and I were online as the Zoom window opened, and all the FAA safety inspectors were in their respective home offices. It wasn't ominous or scary at all. It was the same level of informality as the first meeting, so this was just another conversation, except this conversation turned out to be an incredible testimony for Christ and the work He had planned for Invisible Angels.

"Mr. Greenfield, we have determined that your actions resulted from an honest oversight of the 135 regulations, and there was no intent to purposefully or willingly conduct a noncompliant air-charter operation. We are closing the compliance action against you, recommending you take the following training, and informing you that Invisible Angels must become a Part 135 direct air carrier to continue operations."

The call lasted about fifteen minutes. Genesis 50:20 started racing through my mind. What they meant for evil, God meant for good.

Ed was shocked. "In twenty-five years of practicing aviation law, I have never seen a compliance action closed out in three weeks. This is a miracle, my friend!"

God had provided another miracle in real time amidst the amazing testimony of what He was doing with and through Invisible Angels. We were in the clear, but under heavy restrictions for our operations until we became a Part 135 direct air carrier. As I said before, aviation regulations are quite complex, and significant legal liability is involved when transporting passengers. There was one thing the aviation safety inspector pointed out to all of us during the phone call that none of us had ever realized or considered.

During the call, he stated, "Even though this scenario may be extremely remote, if a trafficking survivor is on one of your flights and, let's say, they change their mind – they can change their mind at any time, before, during, or even after reaching their destination – if this were to happen, you and Invisible Angels could be charged with trafficking, or worse, kidnapping. Even with all the documentation for a planned trip, this would still have to be investigated. This would be a felony and would have to be treated as such. Once you are a Part 135 air carrier, the individual agrees to board the aircraft for the known purpose of transportation, giving you and Invisible Angels legal protection in this area."

This information was a complete surprise, but a much-needed dose of reality. We didn't know this, but God did, and this, in every way, protected us. To grow into the vision God had for us, we needed to become an official air-charter operation. Now, the realities of how this would happen began to emerge.

I called Dave and told him the DC FSDO had closed out the compliance action against me and recommended that Invisible Angels become a Part 135 direct air carrier. I thought I would have to call 9-1-1 to get Dave off the floor. As a former aviation safety inspector, he was more shocked than Ed was.

Now there was a new mountain directly in front of me. How

on earth was this going to happen? What faced us were impossibilities on all sides; it was exactly where God wanted us to be.

CHAPTER 10

EIGHTEEN MONTHS IN THE DESERT

"See, I am doing a new thing! Now it springs up;
do you not perceive it? I am making a way in
the wilderness and streams in the wasteland."
(Isaiah 43:19 NIV)

Dave immediately took the lead on this problem, and although he was pretty negative at times, he was determined to solve it. Me? I was along for the ride. We met at a Vietnamese restaurant a few days after the compliance call ended.

Over bowls of pho, Dave went on, "You'll never be able to do it; I can't see it. The documentation needed is staggering. Your maintenance records must be in perfect order, going back to the year the aircraft was certified, 1980. That's forty years of perfect maintenance records! Do you even have that? You have to write and submit a compliance document explaining how Invisible Angels will comply with every Part 91, 119, and 135 regulation. There are hundreds of regulations you have to explain, in detail, how Invisible Angels will comply. Depending on the operation, those documents are well over a thousand pages long, sometimes more. You have to create hazmat manuals, training manuals, pilot operations manuals, and emergency procedures, and you have to pass a Part 135 oral exam and a check ride. You also have to know those manuals and compliance documents thoroughly. I just can't see this getting done in less than a few years."

I had to remind Dave for whom we and Invisible Angels were working. "Remember the plane?"

"Yes."

"And what just happened the other day?"

"I know."

"So God can't get all this done for us?"

"You don't understand. I know this stuff. This takes years; I just can't see it happening."

I was starting to get mad. I mentally wrote a note to myself to get Dave a new Bible for Christmas because, by the words coming out of his mouth, he had lost his. He was speaking nothing but impossibilities, and I can't stand that. As he was talking, I stopped listening to his speech and just asked God to show him that somehow, Jesus would take care of this.

I silently prayed, and I was looking right at him as he told me it couldn't be done. In a flash, his attitude shifted. I never told him I prayed; I'll wait until he reads this book to find out. Besides, he probably wouldn't have believed me if I had told him. The next words out of his mouth were like a shotgun blast indoors. "Well, if God has gotten you this far, He will take you the rest of the way. God will get this done for you. I don't know how, but He will."

I just smiled and thanked God for instantly answering that prayer.

Invisible Angels was in the clear, but we were still under heavy restrictions if we were to continue operating, and any further operations with passengers, under something called common carriage, would risk another compliance action. Again, aviation regulations are complex. We were stuck between two walls. We couldn't advertise that we were in the business of flying passengers, and able to fly passengers; and if we were to continue flying rescue missions solely for the purpose of flying passengers, then Invisible Angels could not legally pay for the flights. The FAA also views pilots accumulating flight hours as compensation, so I could not legally log any flight hours if Invisible Angels was flying passengers. There were ways around this, but they were very complex.

One option was to partner with other rescue organizations. If we partnered and split the costs of air transportation, fuel, and all other associated costs, we could continue; however, most rescue organizations do not have a budget for that, and this would expose everyone to an enormous amount of liability if anything went wrong. A new partnership with other rescue organizations opens up a whole new level of legal liability for both organizations, neither of which could begin to breach. At every step, we seemed to encounter the same concrete barrier.

Another option was for the pilot in command – me – to pay for the entire cost of the flight: fuel, ramp fees, parking fees, and any maintenance encountered. Then that flight would fall under Part 91 regulations, as long as Invisible Angels is not advertising or implying that it is doing so. I did this for a few flights, but it was very expensive and it exposed Invisible Angels and me to legal liability we could not safely handle. In the first few weeks after the compliance action was closed, we had to turn down multiple rescues, some heartbreaking cases. We could do a few short trips, but the legal liability remained.

Over the next week, Dave and I reviewed every regulation in detail pertaining to flying passengers, and we decided that the safest and wisest course of action was to shut down. God will honor wise decisions. Besides, this was not the only thing

God had planned for Invisible Angels. He had begun to lay out visions for other ministries within Invisible Angels. If God was increasing this ministry, then we would need time to get organized. God had much bigger things in store for us.

We should never try to figure out what God is up to. We cannot. Proverbs 3:5-6 (NIV) says, *Trust in the LORD with all your heart and lean not on your own understanding; in all your ways submit to him, and he will make your paths straight.*

Lean not on your own understanding. Imagine that picture; don't even lean on it. Trying to figure out God's plans is a waste of valuable time, especially when you are in your ultra-late fifties. After coming to many forks in the road during my thirty-five-year walk with Christ, and especially in this season, the only thing to do when God slams on the brakes is to stop along with Him and listen.

Stop everything because God has something to say. He has something to teach you, something to remove from you, and something to prepare you for. You need to be in as much silence as possible to hear the Holy Spirit's prompting. Remember, the Holy Spirit is as sensitive as a dove, and you need to be able to hear Him.

In 1 Kings 19:11-12 (NIV), look back to where God's revelation to Elijah was unveiled: *The LORD said, "Go out and stand on the mountain in the presence of the LORD, for the LORD is about to pass by." Then a great and powerful wind tore the mountains apart and shattered the rocks before the LORD, but the LORD was not in the wind. After the wind there was an earthquake, but the LORD was not in the earthquake. After the earthquake came a fire, but the LORD was not in the fire. And after the fire came a gentle whisper.*

Elijah heard God's voice in the still, small whisper, and now God was telling me it was my turn. I couldn't understand why God started Invisible Angels with a roar, rolling downhill, only to slam on the brakes after nine months. But then, there was the airplane. All I had to do was remember the nine months of nothing between the prophecy of the airplane and watching it land as it was delivered to our airport. I became more comfortable with waiting, and I was hearing God in a new way – completely loud and clear.

Invisible Angels was heading into the desert, but this desert time was also a season of miracles. Looking back, time in the desert is always well spent. That can only be said and understood by crossing the Jordan and looking back from the other side. Desert seasons are not enjoyable, and we cannot see our own growth or what God is doing. It can be a time of painful isolation, but isolation is where we tend to grow the most. God is always with us and always working; it just doesn't always feel like it.

This wasn't my first time heading into the desert, and it certainly won't be my last. There is always growth in the desert, and sometimes problems come to the surface that we wouldn't have seen otherwise. Sometimes we see better in silence.

Even though our missions stopped, the prayer group was still meeting. This was still essential. Even if it appeared nothing was moving, God still was, and we still needed to meet Him there. There needs to be purity in prayer. I am not saying we can only come to Christ in a pure state; obviously, we can never accomplish that. I am saying we need to come to Christ out of a state of empty desperation, seeking only His will and presence. A desperate state where His answer is the only answer we want, because this is the only path that will guide us forward in His will.

For the next few weeks, I was on the phone with anyone at the FAA who could help. At first, I tried to see if an exemption was possible, but the FAA wouldn't even consider that. I called everyone who could explain the process of becoming a

Part 135 air carrier. Everyone I contacted, from other aviation safety inspectors to other Part 135 operators, was extremely helpful and gave me a complete picture of what the process would be like. Dave and I spent hours on Zoom calls where Dave introduced me to many other Part 135 operators. All were supportive and offered to help, but everyone started at the same place: the paperwork. The mountain of documentation had to be completed first.

The process starts with a document called a Preliminary Statement of Intent. Basically, it explains why you want to be a Part 135 air carrier. The FAA wants to know what benefit you will provide to the flying public. This is a simple written explanation of your vision, mission, business model, and how and where you will operate. Once this is accepted (which takes about one to three months), they schedule an initial meeting with everyone involved and begin outlining the entire process. The FAA then provides an Excel spreadsheet of all the items, documents, and steps that must be completed. There are over 350 items. The required documentation is staggering.

Scrolling through the itemized Excel sheet of steps and items needed was daunting. In fact, it was completely overwhelming.

As I said before, Dave is the greatest networker on the planet. He knows everybody. As we were talking about starting the documentation, he said there was another option: "You can pay a company to do the paperwork for you. There is this company I know called Part135.com. They would charge you somewhere in the neighborhood of ten-thousand dollars, but it may be worth it."

Invisible Angels did not have $10,000, but Dave went on. "I know the owner pretty well; let's just call Paul and see what he has to say. Maybe he can help."

Part 135.com is a specialty company that prepares and completes all required documentation for air carriers. They have a very good reputation and have been in business for a long time. Dave called Paul on a lark, and Paul was there as God would have it. He hopped on our Zoom call, and I explained who we were, where we were, and what we were up against. Paul was great – very cheerful and very helpful.

But when he found out Invisible Angels was providing rescue transportation for human trafficking survivors, he shouted – in fact, he screamed – "Human trafficking! What??? You actually provide rescue transportation for human trafficking victims?"

"Yes."

I went on to explain our operations, our rescues, and being caught between a rock and a hard place due to the compliance action.

Paul shouted, "Wait, you really do this?"

"Yes."

"How can I help?"

I started to say, "Well, it would be awesome if –"

He cut me off. "I want to get involved. I want to help. I'll prepare your entire paperwork package for Invisible Angels. Don't worry about anything; I've got you covered. I am not going to take a penny from you."

Dave and I sat frozen. We asked him to repeat that. "Wait, what? You'll do everything for free?"

"Yes."

Dave and I sat stunned. Paul was suddenly in a hurry, as if he wanted to start preparing the package immediately, which he apparently did.

"Look, I'll get everything prepared for you and email the package. There may be some small changes you'll have to make, but you'll have everything you need. You should have it in a few days."

After a thousand thank-yous and a few goodbyes, Paul hopped off the Zoom call. Dave and I just stared at each other.

I didn't know who would speak first. Pinned between shock and awe, we had just witnessed God split the Red Sea again.

Four days later, I had the complete package of paperwork prepared for the FAA. Just over eleven hundred pages of documentation. Everything Invisible Angels needed was there. Through the use of AI and Paul's very creative proprietary programming, Part135.com created a customized compliance package completely specific to the Invisible Angels operation and airplane. It was perfect, precise, and incredibly detailed. In four days, the paperwork and documentation were complete. An absolute miracle.

Over the next few months, I submitted everything to the FAA, and they spent the next eighteen months reviewing it, sending me a few files here and there for small changes, and holding a few meetings to discuss some issues. They were completely satisfied with the documentation, stating it was all in good order. The next steps were my oral exam and flight review.

During the eighteen-month break, I had to prepare. I had to make the transition from a private pilot to a Part 135 pilot – a world I knew nothing about. This was something only Dave could have done. Aviation, and being a pilot, is largely about possessing a certain mentality. Although I held instrument and commercial ratings, a complex, high-altitude, and a few other endorsements, and had around thirteen hundred hours at the time, I had no commercial piloting experience.

When you apply for a job at a small charter airline or a large carrier like United or Southwest, they spend an enormous amount of money and a significant amount of time training you. Some training programs are as long as twenty weeks, some longer, and they are intensive. The training programs introduce you to the world of flying passengers, where much higher safety standards are employed for every aspect of flight. There is a huge transition from being a private pilot with my experience and ratings to a commercial pilot who will be flying passengers. It is a completely different way of thinking. I had no idea what the commercial-piloting world was all about.

Dave knew exactly where I needed to be as a pilot.

Dave saw this long before I ever knew it might become an issue. It wasn't that I didn't know how to fly and operate the aircraft safely; I did that very well. My piloting skills are good; my thinking was the issue. I wasn't thinking like a commercial pilot. Dave had to pound the private pilot out of me and get me thinking and acting like a professional Part 135 pilot. I had no idea what was involved.

You operate the aircraft the same way, but how you think makes the difference. As a private pilot, you stay about ten steps ahead of the airplane at all times. As a commercial pilot, you need to double that, as well as know every regulation involved with your flight operation, and know the aircraft and all of its systems better than you know yourself.

For the next eight Saturdays, Dave and I met in the fancy conference room of a flight school. We knew the owner, and he gave us his blessing to use the space. For nearly sixty hours of instruction, Dave went over every Part 135 regulation and trained me on how Invisible Angels needed to comply. He reviewed every emergency scenario I might encounter: engine fires, low-fuel emergencies, passenger meltdowns, passenger bathroom emergencies, equipment failures, weather-related emergencies, weight and balance issues, airport congestion, navigation and radio failures, pressurization emergencies, and everything else imaginable. Each session lasted between six and eight hours, and by the end of each Saturday, I was spent.

I had taken insurance training for the aircraft, but for the commercial world, I needed complete knowledge and a deep understanding of every system in that airplane. The POH, or *Pilot's Operating Handbook* (the owner's manual) for the P210, is about 250 pages. I needed mastery of every system. A failure in one system will affect others. If the alternator fails in flight, which electronics draw the most amps? How long will I have to run lights and electronics while the aircraft continuously draws down power? How many amp-hours will I have, and which electronics shut down first? What is the order of electrical-equipment shutdown? How will I handle this at night if passengers become anxious? How long will it take to manually pump the gear down if the hydraulic system fails? Will the aircraft remain pressurized if the engine fails? If I lower the engine rpm while descending, will the cabin remain pressurized? If the tires are a little low and it is very hot, what is the maximum landing speed?

The questions went on for weeks. This was critical information I needed to master, and I wasn't enrolled in an airline training program like Southwest or United. This was Dave's training program, customized for Invisible Angels. It worked, and it worked well.

These sessions prepared me for my oral exam with an FAA examiner. Dave went so far as to videotape my responses and then review the videos with me to examine my confidence level. Did I really know the answer, or was I just spitting back a memorized fact? Dave would say, at almost every answer I gave, "Are you asking me or telling me?" This was incredibly painful.

I was a former teacher and have never failed an FAA exam, written or oral, or a check ride. Dave was adamant that I was entering a serious new world where I would have to become a different type of pilot and was unprepared.

He was right. Dave knew the type of training I needed and how to get me there. He was a former chief flight instructor for a major airline and a former aviation safety inspector who gave these check rides. He was also one of the toughest examiners. He beat the private pilot out of me and turned me into a real-world

Part 135 professional commercial pilot. Fourteen months later, I passed my oral exam and check ride perfectly. I never would have been able to do this without Dave. Once again, God had solved this problem and given me a wonderful friend as well.

During every part of this process, God was laying out our path, brick by brick. At every turn where we needed another step accomplished, God was meeting our needs and still delivering miracles in real time; the next one was about to happen.

Airplane hangars are a valuable commodity and about as hard to find as a two-bedroom apartment in the middle of New York City. For most airports, large and small, there is usually a two-year waiting list for hangars. That's exactly what had happened. Two years prior, the same volunteer who had called about the ad for the tug had put his name down on the waiting list for a hangar. He didn't know us, and we didn't know him; in fact, two years earlier, Invisible Angels did not exist. He was just thinking ahead. If he were to buy an airplane, it would be in about two years, and the timing would be right. Turns out it was. God had been, once again, solving our problems upstream.

We needed a new hangar; in fact, we needed a real hangar for the airplane. I was praying for it and had a unique peace about it, but for now, our plane was in an older shade hangar, which is just a covered garage with no walls. It keeps the sun and rain out, but that's about it. No privacy, no security, and no storage space were available, just a covered garage. It would have to do for now, but we would need an actual hangar soon. I knew God would come through, and He did. Like so many answers to prayer, it started with, "One day I got a call . . . ."

I got a call from the airport manager, who knew us well, knew our mission, was a fellow believer, and was amazed at the miracles God was doing for us. There was about to be one more. "Ted, doesn't Bob volunteer for you guys?"

"Yes, he does."

"Well, he put his name on the hangar waiting list back in 2019, and his name came up; we have a hangar available for him. Does he have an airplane?"

"No, not that I know of."

The airport manager called our volunteer Bob, and told him, "If you don't have an airplane, you can give your hangar to Invisible Angels if you want."

In under three minutes, Invisible Angels had an airplane hangar that God had prepared two years earlier. Again, God was continuously solving our problems, providing us with what we needed, and He was about to do it again.

During this preparation time, we were still flying the aircraft, quite a lot actually. We used it to go to conferences and meetings, as well as for other Invisible Angels flights. As I got to know the aircraft better and accumulated more time in it, the VHF radios slowly became a notorious problem. They were forty years old, and although they worked ok, they consisted of forty-year-old technology and badly needed replacement. On one occasion, the radios went silent seconds after takeoff. As I was climbing up, I thought it odd that ATC (air traffic control) was not talking to me. Everything went silent.

I looked over at the radio unit, and it seemed to be ever so slightly sticking out of the panel by maybe a millimeter. I thought this was odd, because everything pretty much sits flush in the panel, so I used my thumb to press the radio hard into the instrument panel. Instantly, all air traffic conversations resumed, beginning with the tower calling out our tail number. Answering promptly and abiding by the tower's departure instructions, the radios worked fine for the rest of the flight, but that airplane was not going up again until a solution was found.

Like everything with airplanes, new radios are expensive. The units themselves cost around $7,000 to $10,000, and another $3,000 to $5,000 is needed for installation. I did not want to fly the airplane again until we had new radios or were on our way to get them.

And then, the next day, we got another call.

One of our volunteers, who is never home on weekdays, happened to be home that day. His landline rang; on the other end was a fellow church member who had heard about Invisible Angels' work. "Hey, I hear you guys are doing incredible work with Invisible Angels. Do you need anything?"

Cautiously, he responded, "Yes, actually, we could use one thousand dollars."

When he told me the story, my eyes popped out of my head, and I jumped. "I hope you asked for more! You have not because you ask not!"

He then went on with the story.

"Is that all you need? One thousand dollars?"

"Well, actually, we need more. Our aircraft radios need to be replaced. We need ten thousand dollars for that, and we need it right away. We don't want to use the aircraft until the radios are replaced."

A very cheerful voice on the other end of the phone said, "Done."

They wrote a check that day. In a matter of hours, after the radios cut out, God had replaced our forty-year-old radios with the latest technology, increasing our safety factor and peace of mind, and immensely satisfying the FAA inspectors.

As the months went on and the paperwork and documentation were submitted, reviewed, and approved, the spreadsheet with over 350 items was slowly being chipped away one by one. Week by week, it went from 350 to 347, then to 330, then to 315, then to 290, then to 265. Once we reached 250, a small light appeared at the end of a long, dark tunnel. Aircraft inspections were being scheduled, maintenance inspections were happening, and we began to round the corner where we could actually imagine receiving our Part 135 air-carrier certificate. One of the biggest hurdles was the annual inspection of our aircraft.

The annual inspection is a mandatory FAA-regulated safety inspection that every aircraft in the United States must undergo, from a small two-seater Cessna to a Boeing 777. The aircraft is essentially taken apart and inspected in great detail for any structural or mechanical issues. It is extremely intensive and is one of the cornerstones of the FAA's safety culture. Annual inspections keep the skies safe by preventing poorly maintained aircraft from ever leaving the ground. It is a valuable safety service for the general public, and can sometimes be very expensive for the aircraft owner.

The safety standards are quite high for general aviation aircraft, such as those owned by a friend. They are even higher for commercial aircraft. An annual inspection for a commercial aircraft cannot be done at any aircraft repair shop; it must be completed by an FAA-regulated Part 145 repair station. This is another inherent safety measure of the FAA that prevents poor maintenance on commercial aircraft. Part 145 repair stations are inspected regularly and randomly, and all employees and mechanics are drug tested regularly and randomly. The general public rarely sees this extraordinary safety measure taken by the FAA. Commercial aircraft maintenance is taken very seriously and is highly regulated.

Commercial aircraft not only have to go through annual inspections, but they also must undergo what is called a one-hundred-hour inspection. Every one-hundred flight hours, the aircraft is inspected again. This is an excellent safety redundancy measure. This applies to every commercial aircraft in the United States, which should make the public feel good about flying on a Delta, Southwest, United, or even a Spirit flight, as well as any chartered aircraft, air ambulance, or cargo plane. Every one hundred hours, or about every three weeks, depending on use, every commercial aircraft is inspected and is either given the *all clear* for service or remains grounded until it is fixed.

All of that applied to us.

As we brought the aircraft in for its annual inspection, I wasn't expecting any surprises. The last annual inspection we completed did not reveal any major issues. Annual inspections are pretty expensive, and our last one was around $4,500, which was cheap for an annual. We knew the commercial annual would be far more extensive and therefore far more expensive. We had budgeted about $12,500 for the inspection, which we thought was about right.

We were way wrong.

The Part 145 repair station would work and bill us in $10,000 increments. This meant that when we delivered the plane for its annual inspection, we put down a $10,000 deposit, and they would send us weekly updates. Annual inspections usually take three to four weeks for smaller shops, as they typically have only one or two people working on the aircraft. The weekly updates began arriving, and we soon realized we might be in trouble. After week four, the bill exceeded our original budget and approached $20,000, causing me distress because the inspection was nowhere near complete – only about 30 percent finished.

Taking a day or two to calm down, I called the maintenance shop to chat with them and hopefully discover they had made a mistake. Knowing we were a small, newly minted nonprofit with a newly minted budget, they explained that although our aircraft was in good shape, it had never undergone a commercial annual inspection. It was a 1980 aircraft, meaning that although all systems functioned well, like the pressurization, oxygen, and hydraulic systems, and just about everything else, they were all forty years old and had timed out according to FAA regulations. Just about every major component on the aircraft needed replacing.

"Okay, so I'll need a realistic number, because we're going to have to raise the money."

"Okay. Realistically, it will be around fifty-five thousand dollars."

Now, I would love to say, "Suddenly, I heard God's voice telling me everything would be all right, and I was instantly consumed by an overwhelming peace as a knock came to my door, followed by someone handing me a forty-five-thousand-dollar check."

No. That didn't happen.

I became completely unglued and wholeheartedly freaked out. For the next few months, I walked through Matthew 14:29-31 (NIV): *"Come," he said. Then Peter got down out of the boat, walked on the water and came toward Jesus. But when he saw the wind, he was afraid and, beginning to sink, cried out, "Lord, save me!" Immediately Jesus reached out his hand and caught him. "You of little faith," he said, "why did you doubt?"*

"I don't know why I freaked out, Lord. I just did, as we all do."

After seeing and walking through all these miracles – from God telling me what I would be doing in this next chapter of my life, to the prophecy about Invisible Angels, to the URL being available for thirty dollars, to the prophecy about the airplane, to the airplane actually being delivered, to the IRS 501(c)(3) being granted in ten days – I took my eyes off of who God was, and stared at the wind and the waves, sinking like a stone. I still don't know why I reacted like this, and it was about to get worse.

Almost overnight, more challenges arose, one being absolutely life-threatening, that would take me to the core of my disbelief. God will take you through levels of your faith that you did not know were there, until you are completely out of options, and the only way you can find a way through is by looking up at God's outstretched hand from under the water.

CHAPTER 11

TELL MY STORY

"They triumphed over him by the blood of the Lamb and by the word of their testimony; they did not love their lives so much as to shrink from death." **(Revelation 12:11 NIV)**

We don't realize how powerful a testimony can be and how powerfully God's Word is used through our testimony. Remember, God's word spoke the universe into existence, so once unleashed, we don't know where it will go or what God will do with it. Consider the description of God's Word in Hebrews 4:12 (NIV): *For the word of God is alive and active. Sharper than any double-edged sword, it penetrates even to dividing soul and spirit, joints and marrow; it judges the thoughts and attitudes of the heart.*

That sounds more like a lightsaber than a sword in our modern-day vernacular. Ephesians 6:17 (NIV) describes God's Word as our primary offensive spiritual weapon: *Take the helmet of salvation and the sword of the Spirit, which is the word of God.*

Our testimony is also something others can relate to, walk

away with, and even see as a missing puzzle piece in the season they may be going through. We have all been in a place where we have been encouraged by someone's testimony, walking away thinking, "If it worked for him, it could work for me." God was about to add a very complex layer to my testimony, one that I could not see coming, that would absolutely stop me in my tracks. For reasons beyond my knowledge and understanding, God had allowed Invisible Angels to be shut down; now it looked like I would be next.

I have never had any significant health issues; in fact, just around the same time as this episode, I was bragging to friends and even the prayer group that I was the only sixty-year-old in Florida who wasn't on any medication. That was about to change. During a routine physical, I had the typical blood work done, and a few days later, I received a phone call from my doctor's office. My blood work had come back abnormal, and they wanted to run some more tests. The word *oncologist* was used. *Wait a minute, this is a cancer doctor! Your machine must be broken; I feel fine, and besides, I am a pilot doing God's work. You clearly have mixed up your patients!*

The word *oncologist* instantly brought fear and panic to every thought I had. Talking with my doctor, I said, "Isn't an oncologist a cancer doctor?"

She said, "Yes, but there really isn't anything to worry about. We just want to take a closer look, and there is nothing urgent. All we need is a closer look."

I think they all say that to calm people down, but it rarely works.

It was also in this season that the prayer team had grown and moved from the small living room into an available room at the church we were attending, and we began to meet regularly on Monday nights. As well as focusing on Invisible Angels, we began to pray for the church and other ministries within it. Still devoted to Invisible Angels, the prayer team became stronger and more determined. We were seeing answers to prayer, not only with Invisible Angels, but throughout our church as well. The prayer team took on an essential new meaning for me, especially when the word *oncologist* was added to my vocabulary.

Within a few months, I found myself at the Florida Cancer Center. Now, the word *cancer* was being used, which shook me to my core. It seems I very quickly went from leisurely witnessing God's miracles and walking through the success of Invisible Angels to sitting in an oncologist's office talking about bone marrow biopsies.

"God, come on, why is this happening now?"

God started speaking a short phrase to me over and over again: "Tell My story. Just tell My story."

For the next two months, we tried changing my diet, removing supplements, adding new supplements, and just about every other possible route to rule out dietary or external factors. My blood work continued to deteriorate.

A few months into seeing the oncologist, he finally said, "We have to seriously consider a bone marrow biopsy."

This struck a serious chord with me because now they were looking for something medically serious. I was terrified, and although I knew God was in control, I kept asking, "Why now?" I asked God over and over again.

God just kept saying the same thing: "Tell My story. Just tell My story."

I did just that, to anyone who would listen.

As I went in to have my bone marrow biopsy done, I was focused on telling God's story and on everything but myself. Although I was pretty sad, afraid, and alone, I knew that if I kept my focus on others and encouraged them, I would not feel any of those depressing feelings that were hovering around me at the time. It was an early appointment, and I didn't want to set anyone back by having them drop me off at the hospital at 5:00 a.m. I took an early Uber to the hospital, and on the drive in, I sensed that God was completely supporting me.

Being led into the intake nurse's office at about 5:30 that morning, a very pleasant lady sat down in front of me. She was about my age and started entering all my information into her iPad before the procedure. As I told her my birth date, she just sighed, as if she had just heard some bad news.

I immediately shot back with a surprised and somewhat angry look, but still with a smile, and said, "What was that for? What's the matter? Why the sigh?" as if I were a very good friend, able to take that liberty with her.

She sighed again and said, "Well, I'm just right behind you and feeling old."

I kind of got mad, but I shot back with the same huge, smirky smile. "Let me tell you something. More has happened to me in the last five years than at any other time in my life, and I will tell you a story."

I started to enthusiastically lecture her way too early, and before she had had an adequate amount of coffee to deal with me. Over the next thirty minutes, I told her the entire story of Invisible Angels. When I finished, with a big fat smile on my face and a joyous shout, I said, "What are you sad for? I'm telling you right now, God has an amazing plan for you, and I'm the one who is about to get a hole drilled through his pelvis."

She sat there and looked at me, paused for a couple of seconds, and then a single tear of joy rolled down her cheek. With cheerful tears, she said, "You've inspired me so much. You have no idea."

We went on to talk about what God was doing in her life, and at that moment, the feelings of sadness, fear, and loneliness vanished. I just saw what God was doing through me. "Tell My story." That's all I had to do.

She walked me into pre-op and handed me off to a couple of nurses who put me into a fluorescently lit but very comfortable bed, complete with warm sheets, and they began prepping me for the procedure. IVs went in, and then they gave me something to take the edge off. To be completely honest, I would have gladly paid extra for that.

As I got more and more comfortable and my mood improved, they wheeled me into the operating room, which, in my state, looked like Kylo Ren's (from *Star Wars*) personal interrogation room.

Then, injecting something into my IV and with a smirky smile, as if they had a big secret, they said, "You are going to feel pretty good in a few seconds."

And I certainly did. The last thing I remembered was asking them if they could put on some music and then saying, "Hey, do you want to hear a story?"

I woke up in the recovery room feeling pretty good, no pain, and was still in a great mood! I can't remember what I said; I was probably telling them about Invisible Angels, but most likely I had fire trucks mixed up with airplanes, puppies instead of people, and I am sure there was a unicorn and balloons in there somewhere. All I remember is that I was talking, and all the nurses were laughing. Whatever they gave me to put me to sleep must have still been working.

As the medication wore off and I was taken back home to sleep, the next week was spent entering a new phase in a spiritual battle. It wasn't the typical spiritual battle, where it is one-on-one and you know what the Enemy wants; this was more like an undersea battle between two submarines. I love submarine movies: *The Hunt for Red October, Hunter Killer, Crimson Tide, Run Silent, Run Deep,* and *U-571.* The list goes on. Submarine battles in movies can illustrate our spiritual battles with the Enemy of our souls very well. A battle to the death, where one cannot see the other, and the only way to find out what the Enemy is doing is to sit perfectly still and listen in absolute silence. This is the Ephesians 6 battle we face day by day, and when you are taking ground for the kingdom, make no mistake: the Enemy will fight back, and fight back hard. The Enemy wants one outcome only: your death.

The prayer team had been praying for me this entire time, and God had been leading me in a personal course of prayer through healing Scriptures and speaking in tongues. But this seemed deeper – something I had never experienced before, a new type of spiritual attack requiring a different kind of battle. A battle where I couldn't see the Enemy, and I had to fight from a spiritual place of absolute silence, listening purposefully and intently. I had to hear God's slightest whisper to battle with every Scripture-sword He called me to use. This was also new training, because the stakes were high. This could medically affect me for life.

Of course, I thought about the worst outcome. Bone marrow biopsies are looking for cancer, and I took this directly to God. In church, during worship, I had a prayerful conversation with God. I am not afraid to die. He knows that, and I know that. I just asked for one thing, if that were the case: please don't drag it out. Make it quick. I know where I am going, and spending eternity with Christ in heaven is an awesome thought. But Lord, I really want to see this ministry out. I want to experience what you are going to do with Invisible Angels. It's almost like it's not fair to start it and then be called home before we cross over the Jordan into the promised land.

I am sure Moses felt the same thing.

Two days later, I was waiting in one of the exam rooms at the Florida Cancer Center to get the results. The doctor walked in smiling. "You're going to die one day, but not from this. No cancer, no leukemia."

I instantly felt 150 pounds lighter and felt an immediate answer to prayer. I would get to see what God is going to do with this ministry! Praise God! The prayer team rejoiced and praised God, but an issue still remained. My numbers were still taking a nosedive, and they couldn't figure out why. To further confuse the situation and give me cause to think this was entirely a spiritual attack, I had no symptoms: no weird bleeding, no bruising, and my energy level was bursting through the roof as usual. The doctor said I should be feeling tired, should have red dots all over my skin, and should be bruising or bleeding. My numbers went down to frightfully low territory; however, I still felt fine, and there were absolutely no symptoms. Out of options, the doctors suggested a round of chemotherapy.

A week later, I found myself seated in a comfortable recliner chair in a chemotherapy ward. Every Wednesday for a month, I sat for eight hours with an IV in my arm, receiving infusions. The entire time I was there, I heard God tell me repeatedly, "Tell My story. Tell My story. Tell My story."

I did. I told the Invisible Angels story to everyone around me.

I saw the amazement on people's faces as I told the story of how God had created this aviation ministry and the miracles that had happened. I was still in the middle of the forest and couldn't see the trees, but I knew God was working. I could see the impact He was having at that very moment of telling the story, and I knew He was doing something in every person I told the story to. What He was going to do with that, I will probably never know; all I had to do was my part. God had placed me in the cancer center, in the chemo ward, in the intake office, and in this entire situation with specific instructions to tell His story. Maybe this whole medical episode would go away when everyone heard what God wanted them to hear? God kept telling me, "Tell My story."

The chemo didn't work, which I had a feeling it wouldn't.

From the beginning, I felt it was a waste of the insurance company's money and my time. They tried steroids, which were miserable and didn't work either. Then they tried a new drug, and my numbers came back up and stabilized. Finally, after several months, something worked. For the next two months, my numbers stabilized into the normal range, and although I was rejoicing, and the prayer team was rejoicing, one obstacle remained and could ground me for life. My diagnosis was a *no-fly* item. Having this issue would disqualify me from getting my FAA medical certificate, leaving me unable to fly. This was serious.

You can't get around FAA medical certification, and that is a good thing. No one wants unhealthy pilots flying planes. Simply not reporting this condition was not an option after seeing all the miracles God had done up to this point. That would be a real *Jacob* move. I could not turn around, create a lie, and then stand on that lie and expect God to honor this ministry.

But to tell you the truth, I thought about it. Reporting this condition was terrifying. Again, I stared at the wind and the waves and listened to Jezebel's threats over God's promises, and I started to sink again. Then Jesus stretched out His hand.

I started researching and preparing for my upcoming medical exam when I found an updated FAA-approved medication list. Sure enough, my medication had been approved several months earlier. It seemed I was in the clear.

I scheduled my appointment with my FAA medical examiner and went in a few days later. Of course, I told him about the Invisible Angels story, but he was completely disinterested. He was all business. He performed the usual vision, color blindness, and diabetes tests, as well as checked my blood pressure, heart rate, weight, and other vitals. I am 5 feet, 11 inches, 175 pounds, with a blood pressure of 119/70 and a resting heart rate of sixty-five. All pretty good. Then, a thorough physical exam was followed by a discussion of any new medications or health events. This is where it got scary.

I told him my diagnosis, and he pulled up the FAA worksheet for aviation medical examiners to follow for this condition. He then looked at section 5 of the worksheet, under *Treatment.* He said, "You can't be on any medicine or treatment for this."

"But have a look at the approved list. This medication is on it."

He was using last year's form, the one he had in his hand. He looked at me and said, "I'm sorry, I can't issue you your medical certificate. I'm going to have to defer this to the chief FAA medical examiner in Oklahoma City."

My heart sank. I said again, "The medicine I am on is approved by the FAA. It was approved a few months ago." He looked it up on his computer, and sure enough, it was approved, but he still needed to defer this to the chief medical examiner in Oklahoma City. My heart sank deeper. He said, "Don't worry; I'm going to call the chief medical examiner for you. I want you to go home and relax. Don't worry about anything, and I'll call you in an hour."

I walked out of his office feeling very hopeful, except that the reality of not having a medical certificate was like a wet bag of sand on my shoulders. From that moment on, I could not pilot an aircraft. I drove down to the beach to do a prayer walk, where I walked up and down the beach for about an hour, prayed, and gave it to God. "You have this, and I can do nothing to affect the outcome."

About an hour later, my phone rang, and the FAA medical examiner said he spoke to the medical examiner in Oklahoma City, and they should be able to issue me a special issuance clearance, which means I will be able to fly. The only question is when. The FAA is a huge government organization where nothing happens fast. With all the miracles I have seen and the knowledge that God firmly has Invisible Angels in His control and grip, I knew I would get my medical clearance in God's perfect timing, not mine.

Now I'd entered a new phase where God was stretching me, teaching me, and inviting me deeper into His Word. It was paralyzing knowing I could do nothing to change, affect, or move this situation. As an FAA employee, it would be highly frowned upon if I called the medical branch and tried to hurry this up, and I really felt God telling me not to. If I were to do that, I might end up at the very bottom of the pile because they cannot show special favoritism to their employees. I was like one of the many pilots out there with a medical issue. Now it was time to do every living Christian's favorite thing: wait.

Simultaneously undergoing bone marrow biopsies and chemotherapy, the airplane was still undergoing its annual inspection, and the weekly updates were slowly climbing. We were inching toward the original verbal estimate of $55,000. Donations had come in to cover $20,000, but the wind and waves started to overtake me, and all I could see was that Invisible Angels was now close to $35,000 in debt for FAA-required aircraft repairs.

We all come to these places in our faith walk. This can be where God gently guides us on handling it, like in Matthew 17:19-21 (NIV): *Then the disciples came to Jesus in private and asked, "Why couldn't we drive it out?" He replied, "Because you have so little faith. Truly I tell you, if you have faith as small as a mustard seed, you can say to this mountain, 'Move from here to there,' and it will move. Nothing will be impossible for you."*

Faith has an elasticity to it like a big rubber band. God will stretch your faith through trials to unbelievably huge levels, transforming that rubber band into something much longer and stronger. After the trial, hopefully, your faith will never return to its original size. It's the longer, stronger version.

After the trial, it is also key to remember what God did and how He applied your faith to your circumstances. When we come upon a new scenario that needs longer, stronger faith, we must remember what God did and stand on that as a promise for seeing us through in the future. Standing on what God has done for us shows us God's character, what He has done, His promises, and most importantly, who He is. God was about to give me another reminder of who He is and how important Invisible Angels was, in the shape of an aircraft propeller.

Aircraft maintenance is very complex. It's not like fixing a car, where you bring it to a shop for repairs. With aircraft, parts are removed and shipped to other companies for repair or rebuilding. The propeller for our aircraft was sent separately for overhaul. Aircraft propellers can be quite complicated: three blades, all with variable pitch, about six feet in diameter, and each blade can be heated for ice and snow conditions.

The original estimate we discussed with the maintenance company did not include the propeller overhaul, which I did not know. Amid comfortable recliner chairs and chemotherapy, an email arrived from the propeller company with a bill for $4,750. I was thrilled, as I expected it to be far higher; I have seen propeller bills close to $20,000! I called the propeller shop to see if they had submitted the bill to the maintenance company and if it was included in the original estimate. They said, "No, we bill separately; we need payment now."

We had a little over $700 in our business account. I asked them for a few days to make the payment, and with a very cheerful response, the woman on the other end of the phone said, "Absolutely, no problem! We were curious about what you do because you have a cool name, so we looked at your website, and we think what you are doing is amazing!"

Smiling like a Cheshire cat, I said, "Want to hear a story?" "Sure!"

I told her the Invisible Angels story and what God had done, and she was blown away and very happy that they were able to help us. She said, "No worries. We can give you a couple of weeks. You guys are doing awesome work!"

I hung up the phone and just prayed, "God, this is entirely on you. We only have seven hundred dollars."

The two weeks passed, and nothing happened. No sudden donations, no breakthroughs, just silence. I knew God was going to provide, but it literally was driving me crazy and keeping me up at night. I can't stand bills not being paid, and I was very concerned about Invisible Angels acquiring a reputation for not paying its bills on time, while simultaneously being very aware that everyone would be able to see God providing a financial breakthrough for us. I was in a new place in my faith journey, clearly being stretched to new levels.

Two weeks later, to the day, an email popped up from the propeller shop, a simple reminder that the invoice was due. Gasping at the email and wondering where the money would come from, I pushed my chair back from my desk and left for a walk to burn off energy and pray. Almost reflexively, and without expectation, I grabbed my keys and headed for the mailbox. Trying to think of anything else, I opened the box, collected the mail, and returned to the house. Flipping through it, I found a blank envelope to Invisible Angels with an unknown return address. Opening the envelope, I saw the familiar perforated edge of a check and froze. I stopped and stared. Inside was a donation for $5,000.

God is never late.

Now, I have to be honest and admit that I was also partly bummed. There was a zero missing from that check. I wanted a check for $50,000 to make all these problems go away, so we could get on with our ministry, get the airplane back, and get on with doing God's work. God had other plans; He still wanted me to *tell His story.*

Just a few days after I paid the propeller bill, I had a routine medical procedure scheduled that everyone over fifty gets about every five years – an entirely unnatural but necessary procedure involving small cameras on flexible tubes. I went in and was greeted by a wonderful, kind staff, received the same heated blankets and very similar medication that improved my mood, my faith, made me better-looking, much more confident, and outright enjoyable to talk to. An in-and-out procedure, I was home a few hours later, comfortably and reluctantly letting the medication wear off.

Later that afternoon, a fever suddenly spiked, and within a few hours, I was feeling absolutely lousy. Calling the doctor's office, I was told to go directly to the emergency room. Hopping in my car, I had no idea what could be wrong. Within a few minutes of checking into the emergency room, my clothes were off, I was laid flat on a gurney (without heated blankets), and I was being rolled down a very cold hallway to be scanned and given an MRI. It all happened so fast, and I felt so lousy that I didn't have time to worry. Within twenty minutes, I was being admitted to the hospital for the weekend with no real explanation.

The next morning, a few doctors came in and out of my room, checking on me, asking questions, doing their normal doctor stuff. They said they were waiting for the surgeon to see me.

Surgeon? What's the problem? Did a piece of the camera fall off? What is happening? How did I go from resting comfortably at home to lying in a hospital bed waiting for surgeons within twenty-four hours?

About an hour later, the surgeon came into the room – quite young-looking, actually – and very cheerfully and kindly introduced herself. I thought she must be fifteen, but maybe that is a result of my approaching sixty. Everyone looks like a high school sophomore. She explained that I needed to have a ten- to twelve-inch section of my lower intestine removed.

Completely switching my mood to crisis management, I

listened intently to her description of the situation and just took it all in without reaction. She told me they wanted to keep me in the hospital for another night and reassured me that this surgery did not need to happen today, but it needed to happen sometime in the near future. Then she started talking about the percentage of risk of having a colostomy bag. She was very kind and probably was just doing her job, based on a set of scans taken the previous day, but clearly, this did not make the least bit of sense. "God, You have the last word here."

A few hours later, another surgeon, just as young-looking, came into my room and explained the exact same thing: colostomy bag percentages and all. After he left, a sense of peaceful resistance came over me. That's the only way I can explain it. I wasn't mad; I knew in my soul they were wrong, and I knew there was nothing wrong with me, but something had happened to put me in the hospital.

Released on Sunday afternoon, I went to the prayer-team meeting Monday night and told them the whole story. Spiritual attacks can take on any form, and this certainly felt like one. Too sudden, too damaging, and with no rational explanation, a medical procedure of this magnitude would have sidelined me for weeks and might have left me permanently medically compromised. We prayed feverishly over Invisible Angels and me for the rest of the evening. The next morning, I called my general doctor and told her what had happened. She wanted me to come in right away.

A member of the prayer team gave me some wise advice: Everything is spiritual, but you can't spiritualize everything. That certainly is true. Although this was an obvious spiritual attack, doctors still needed to be involved, and the right questions needed to be asked.

After hearing what happened, my doctor wanted me to see a well-known surgeon in the area, who had one of the best reputations in the state. Agreeing that this was a wonderful idea, I called to make an appointment. The earliest opening was in two months, but just as she was about to hang up the phone, she said, "Wait, there is a cancellation. Can you be here tomorrow morning?"

"Yes!"

Now that's God!

The next morning, I found myself waiting in the exam room. Quickly opening the door, the new *super-surgeon* greeted me cheerfully. "Hey! What's up? What happened?"

I told him about my weekend in the hospital as he pulled up my scans and MRIs on his laptop. Then he looked more closely at the images, played around with his laptop for a bit, looked more closely, and stopped.

He turned directly to me and said, "I would not perform this surgery. You do not need to have this done. It looks like there was a small problem during your colonoscopy. Sometimes these are difficult to spot. Don't have this surgery. You don't need it."

He closed his laptop, smiled, shook my hand, and left the room. I didn't even have time to ask him if he wanted to hear a story.

In under seven minutes, I got the reason for my weekend stay in the hospital: a mistake during my procedure. Sure enough, a few days later, I met with the doctor who performed the procedure, and he all but admitted that he must have clipped something, and it quickly became infected. The look on his face was enough; there would be no need for threats or lawsuits. Besides, I was perfectly fine now and have been fine ever since.

And I still had a story to tell.

CHAPTER 12

RUNNING UPHILL

*"I have told you these things, so that in me you
may have peace. In this world, you will have
trouble. But take heart! I have overcome the
world."* (John 16:33 NIV)

In case you haven't figured this out yet, from the moment you
accepted Christ as your Lord and Savior, your entire Christian
walk will be uphill all the way. And if God actually calls you
into ministry, or to start one, then get your running shoes on.
You are about to enter a million-mile marathon, uphill the
whole way.

From the moment God created and called me into Invisible
Angels, I had visions of flying survivors to safety; transforming
lives; speaking at churches and conferences; raising awareness
of the human trafficking issue; becoming part of an amazing
network of rescue organizations; and growing Invisible Angels
beyond rescue and recovery operations to provide mentoring,
donated vehicles, fund college or trade school tuition for survivors, and be part of a dynamic community raising up survivors

to reach their full potential while simultaneously making a massive dent in the human trafficking issue.

The reality was a bit different.

Three years into Invisible Angels, I was facing: almost being shut down by the FAA, a cancer scare, a newly acquired blood disorder that could permanently disqualify me from flying, and a weekend requiring the removal of a foot-long section of my digestive system. I was leading a newly formed ministry, responsible for $35,000 in federally mandated aircraft repairs and an additional $12,000 in new expenses before Invisible Angels could even reach a runway. Once those bills were paid, each flight would cost between $3,000 and $4,000. After three years and multiple rescue flights, I faced insurmountable obstacles: a disassembled airplane in an FAA maintenance facility, $50,000 in expenses, and an annual budget exceeding $360,000.

Invisible Angels had $720 in the bank.

I am a positive, optimistic, passionate, messianic, born-again believer, and God was taking me right up to, and over, the cliff of my belief. These were serious mountains that needed to be moved, and doubt started slowly creeping into my thoughts.

During the midst of these mounting bills and pressures, I was sitting in my office with a friend when another bill popped up in my inbox. I saw the amount, just stared at it for a second, and, exhaling through exhaustion, I said, "Where is all this going to come from?" Asking that question was the moment I took my eyes off God, looked at the wind and the waves, and started to sink.

What I wasn't looking at was:

- God telling me my next season would be in aviation ministry,

- God telling me to buy the domain name *Invisible Angels,*

- God telling me to write a budget for an organization that didn't exist,

- God providing a donated six-passenger airplane before we even had a bank account, a website, or business cards,

- Being in the middle of the process of the FAA certifying Invisible Angels to become a Part 135 direct air carrier,

- All our documentation being done for free and completed in less than a week,

- A 501(c)(3) approval in eight days via snail mail,

- All the initial funds coming in from a single three-minute YouTube post,

- And most importantly, the absolute, indisputable witness, evidence, and promise that God created Invisible Angels, and this is what He, not I, will finish.

Invisible Angels is His ministry, and although I was involved, this wasn't my fight.

That is very easy to read and very hard to walk through.

Look at Paul. From the instant he heard Jesus say, *"Why do you persecute me?"* in Acts 9:4 (NIV), every event in Paul's life was uphill. Not once did Paul get to coast. Jesus made Paul's path clear when He told the reluctantly argumentative Ananias to go to an address on Straight Street in Acts 9:15-16 (NIV): *But the Lord said to Ananias, "Go! This man is my chosen instrument to proclaim my name to the Gentiles and their kings and to the people of Israel. I will show him how much he must suffer for my name."*

Did he ever.

In Acts 22, during one of Paul's early sermons, the crowd

intently listened to his testimony until verse 22 (NIV): *The crowd listened to Paul until he said this. Then they raised their voices and shouted, "Rid the earth of him! He's not fit to live!"*

Everything was fine until they wanted to kill him! And it did not improve from there. Beaten over and over again, shipwrecked, and consistently chased, harassed, mocked, arrested, and imprisoned, Paul's entire ministry was an uphill marathon, and it did not end with a victorious crossing of the finish line and a statue of him in Jerusalem. It ended with the thud of his head falling into a basket. Eleven others met a similar end.

Why is our walk so difficult?

We are no longer of the world from the moment we accept Christ. We have a new nature that goes against the grain of the world. It is uphill both ways. In John 3:3 (NIV), *Jesus replied, "Very truly I tell you, no one can see the kingdom of God unless they are born again."*

From the instant the Holy Spirit took residence in you, it was a rebirth; you were born again with an entirely new nature. That's why Jesus referred to this spiritual event as being *born again.*

Paul, who had a radical salvation experience, describes this metamorphosis to the entire Corinthian church in 2 Corinthians 5:17 (NIV): *Therefore, if anyone is in Christ, the new creation has come: The old has gone, the new is here!*

You are a new creation in Christ, with a new outlook, perspective, and heavenly-spiritual understanding of the physical world we live in. As Jesus stated in John 3:3, you can now *see* the kingdom of God. The rest of the world is unable to. Possessing this new outlook sets us up to see an entire realm of extraordinary, supernatural possibilities, and that includes heavenly miracles!

When I accepted Christ in the late 1980s, the very first spiritual revelation I had was all the people who would spend eternity apart from Christ because they had rejected His call to salvation. That kept me awake at night for the first few years of my Christian walk.

From the moment I accepted Christ, I instantly saw reality and the physical world we live in through the spiritual lens of Christ and the Holy Spirit. That literally rearranged my DNA. Jesus explains this in one of His most intense prayers, the night before His execution, in John 17:16-18 (NIV): *"They are not of the world, even as I am not of it. Sanctify them by the truth; your word is truth. As you sent me into the world, I have sent them into the world."*

Although we have a new spiritual lens and perspective, we still live here, and it is an uphill struggle. Some days we do our best just to tread water and stay afloat, and other days we walk on the water. After thirty-five years of walking with Christ, maintaining that perspective is still often difficult.

Bill Johnson has a good remedy to maintain your outlook: "You have to remember God's last miracle and pray from that perspective."

When I started to look at what Invisible Angels was facing through a worldly lens, I would buckle under the pressure of facing impossible circumstances. But once I viewed the situation from the perspective of God's promises and past miracles, I would quickly see God solving our problems through a matrix of endless possibilities and solutions; some problems were solved by God placing us in the very predicament to begin with.

At this point, I had no medical certificate, which meant I could not legally fly an airplane. The Invisible Angels' aircraft was in an FAA-certified maintenance facility, disassembled, undergoing a very extensive and expensive annual inspection, and now Invisible Angels was presented with another financial crisis. If you are surprised by car or homeowners' insurance, you must sit down for commercial aircraft insurance. Just imagine what Delta, American, Southwest, or United pay to insure their airplanes. It is in the millions. Commercial aircraft insurance is extremely expensive, and very few companies provide it. After a thorough search, our insurance broker found only one company in the United States that would insure Invisible Angels, and the annual premium would be $25,000.

Twelve-thousand dollars was due now.

Although the insurance bill was due, the Invisible Angels' airplane was in a maintenance shop, parked, disassembled, and being conformed to FAA Part 135 safety standards. It didn't need insurance because it wasn't going anywhere or doing anything. I called the insurance company and explained the situation, and they said, "No problem; we don't need you to pay anything right now."

They couldn't even insure the airplane until it had completed the FAA inspection. That was at least four to five weeks away! Problem solved. The issue was still there, but the urgency was gone, and the immediate problem was solved. I realized everything would be an impossible emergency unless I started looking at every event from God's perspective. God had called us into this arena, He provided the airplane, and He would give us everything we needed to fight the battle. Exodus 14:14 (NIV) says, *"You need only to be still."* God will equip us for what He has called us into.

God's solutions rarely, if ever – well, really never – conform to our logic. Isaiah contains some of the most beautiful prophetic promises in the entire Bible, but specifically in chapters 40 to 55. In Isaiah 55:8-9 (NIV) God says, *"For my thoughts are not your thoughts, neither are your ways my ways," declares the* Lord. *"As the heavens are higher than the earth, so are my ways higher than your ways and my thoughts than your thoughts."*

God's solutions are outside our realm, perspective, and concept of time.

I was struggling to keep my eyes fixed on God's promises

while staring at bills coming in with no way to pay them. I had great peace in meeting with the prayer team every Monday night, but it seemed like Invisible Angels was stuck. There were no solutions on the horizon, and no promises of major donations. A stable amount came in every month, but it wasn't nearly enough to cover everything. We had written several grants, totaling more than we needed, but all of them were rejected over the next few weeks. Sometimes God will put you in a place where you have no other option but to sit and listen. This is exactly where He wants you, because spiritual strength is developed through silence and struggle.

There is a state park near my house in the Tampa area that is over eighteen thousand acres, with miles of hiking trails and an eight-mile paved loop going through some of the most beautiful Florida scenery and wildlife imaginable. This was an amazing place to walk and pray, and it turned into a daily two-hour prayer walk. Calling it my Emmaus walk, I would walk about four miles every morning just before sunrise, and I would listen and pray. I was in good company. Jesus did the same thing in Mark 1:35 (NIV): *Very early in the morning, while it was still dark, Jesus got up, left the house and went off to a solitary place, where he prayed.*

Jesus needed the silence and solitude to hear His Father, and I started hearing God in the same way. I started to gain the peace that transcends all understanding in Philippians 4:7. You need silence and solitude to hear God. Not saying He only speaks to you in times of silence and solitude, but it is the silence and solitude that tunes your ear to Him, enabling you to hear.

I started getting into a new rhythm of hearing God. It wasn't so much the panic starting to subside as it was God pulling me back up from under the water. God was showing up in new and different ways, showing me He had never left in the first place. God was still living inside the problems Invisible Angels faced.

One night, driving to a dinner party, I was still consumed with the approaching maintenance bills, and a new problem had popped up. The individual handling our accounting had left Invisible Angels. I failed accounting three times in college, and the instructor only released me on my third try after I begged and pleaded with her to pass me. She did, only after I promised that I would never have anything to do with accounting in my professional life. Nearly forty years later, I had no intention of breaking that promise. Then I heard God softly say, "I am making the plane perfect."

Like air being let out of a balloon, my anxiety dissolved. If He is making the plane perfect, He will pay for it. If it's God's will, it's God's bill. I just laughed and said out loud, "Thank You, Lord. Now I need some accounting help." There was peace after that. I smiled during the rest of the drive to the dinner party.

Ray and his wife Monica host a small social group called The Monthly Supper Club from Radiant Church in the Tampa area. I had been going to several small groups at Radiant and truly enjoyed this one. With a lovely group of people getting together every month for a potluck, there were always new people joining and some people leaving. That night, God led me to meet someone special.

Scattered throughout the house and backyard, about twenty of us enjoyed the food everyone brought. A couple of people knew about Invisible Angels and asked how things were going. I told them we were becoming a Part 135 air carrier, undergoing an extensive inspection, and that we had some *opportunities for support,* remaining as positive as possible about our financial situation without asking anyone for money. A woman named Maria a few chairs away perked up and said, "So what does your ministry do?"

"We provide air rescue and recovery transportation for human trafficking survivors."

She thought this was fascinating and wanted to hear more. I told her the story of Invisible Angels. She listened intently and loved it, and we talked a bit more. I told her about my health scare and that I was now waiting for medical clearance. She said, "He hasn't brought you this far just to fail. He is still here. He will make a way for you."

Smiling, I agreed and thanked her.

Then she said, "Is there any way I can help? Do you need volunteers?"

"Sure. What do you do?"

"I'm an accountant."

Those three words brought me face-to-face with God's love, grace, gentleness, and an overwhelming awareness that God is living inside our problems. Our worrying or whining can be insulting to our God, who loves us so unfathomably much that when we worry and whine about our issues, we are unable to see how He actually solves them.

God solves our problems upstream, just as He did when the Israelites were crossing the Jordan in Joshua 3:16 (NIV). *The water from upstream stopped flowing. It piled up in a heap a great distance away, at a town called Adam in the vicinity of Zarethan, while the water flowing down to the Sea of the Arabah (that is, the Dead Sea) was completely cut off. So the people crossed over opposite Jericho.*

As they crossed the Jordan, the water did not pile up where they were crossing; it piled up twenty miles upstream in Adam, where the Israelites could not see it. I saw this in real time repeatedly.

In the middle of all these micro-miracles, I still had a full-time job at the FAA to tend to. I had just completed a project for another pilot safety group, and the project lead, Trina, had heard about Invisible Angels and the work we had done and was really interested in hearing more. I went on to tell the story of how God was still creating miracles even when we were parked in a maintenance facility in pieces.

When it came to telling her about the issue of my medical certificate being under review by the chief medical examiner, she jumped in. "I have a friend who works there; you should give her a call."

The flight examiner's office in Oklahoma City presides over all 770,000 pilots in the United States and all their medical issues. Calling to see if they had a form with my name on it and when it would be reviewed and approved would be like looking for a specifically shaped grain of sand on a beach. I called anyway.

I love making calls on Teams or Zoom. Being able to see the other person instantly reveals who you are talking to and whether they are happy to hear from you. Trina's friend answered the Teams call right away.

"Hi, I am Ted Greenfield. Trina suggested you may be able to help me; she said I should call you to see if you could let me know the status of my medical certificate."

I went on to explain the situation, and I gave her all the necessary details. She spent the next minute or so searching on her computer.

"I can call you back if you need time. I really appreciate your help!" I said.

"No need, Mr. Greenfield. It is right here. It will take a few weeks to get mailed out because we are backed up, but I can email you a copy. It was approved yesterday. You are good to go!"

With uncontainable excitement, I asked, "Do you want to hear a story?"

For the next twenty minutes, I told her the Invisible Angels' story about how God started everything. She was in awe and wanted to hear more. She was amazed and loved the fact that she was there to answer this call.

Clicking off the Teams call, she said, "If you have this problem next year, call me, and I can get it processed for you right away."

In just a few seconds, I was overjoyed, staring at a blank monitor, realizing I had just witnessed another Joshua 3:16 moment. "It was approved yesterday" was playing through my mind on a loop. I can legally fly a plane again.

God was starting to turn us around the corner.

Over the next few days, the long Excel spreadsheet of over 350 items to complete dwindled to little more than a hundred. Our certificate was finally in sight; the only things standing between us and operational status were about six weeks and $50,000.

During this entire season, for the past five years, God has been waking me up at 3:00 a.m. and speaking to me. It's still happening today; between 3:00 and 4:30 a.m. have been some of the most incredible prayer times and revelations from God, all in the middle of the night. I've often wondered why 3:00 a.m., but I now know I am not alone.

When I shared this with others, I discovered God wakes a lot of people up at exactly the same time, and there are all sorts of reasons, but the one that stood out so plainly to me was that, at this hour, my mind is completely stripped of every logical task, thought, and function. I can hear God perfectly because He's the only one there, and I'm not distracted. God and my pillow are the only things I'm leaning on at 3:00 a.m.

In that still, silent state, I heard God say, "Fill your jars with oil."

I knew the story in 2 Kings 4:2-7 (NIV):

> *Elisha replied to her, "How can I help you? Tell me, what do you have in your house?" "Your servant has nothing there at all," she said, "except a small jar of olive oil." Elisha said, "Go around and ask all your neighbors for empty jars. Don't ask for just a few. Then go inside and shut the door behind you and*

*your sons. Pour oil into all the jars, and as each is
filled, put it to one side." She left him and shut the
door behind her and her sons. They brought the jars
to her and she kept pouring. When all the jars were
full, she said to her son, "Bring me another one."
But he replied, "There is not a jar left." Then the oil
stopped flowing. She went and told the man of God,
and he said, "Go, sell the oil and pay your debts. You
and your sons can live on what is left."*

This widow was completely out of options. Facing the confisca-
tion of her two sons, a common consequence of ninth-century
B.C. debt, the widow had no means to pay off her husband's
bills, or so she thought. She only saw a little olive oil in front of
her, but God saw something much bigger; she had everything
she needed.

Books and sermons have been written on these fourteen
sentences, and they don't even begin to uncover what is there.
Whether the olive oil represents your faith, or only what you
have at the time, or what God can do with what we give Him,
it always ends with a multiplying miracle, and it was repeated
a couple of times, nine hundred years later, with some baskets
and a few fish.

I was familiar with the widow's predicament.

With just under $800 in the Invisible Angels' bank account,
and facing a $10,000 maintenance payment due in a few days,
the only thing left to do was to give it to God. It simply wasn't
there, or so I thought.

The prayer team was praying for a financial miracle, and
I was praying for a financial miracle, except I really wasn't
praying. I started to worry again, which is just complaining,
or even worse, the reverse of faithful prayer. I didn't completely
understand the instructions either. I stopped whatever I had to

do that morning and read 2 Kings chapter 4 about eleven times, listened to a number of sermons throughout the day, and still didn't get it. It was a riddle I couldn't figure out. I was praying, asking God, "What and where are my jars?"

Sometimes God will give you a riddle as an invitation to lean into Him, to search Him out, to seek His Word. Like following a trail of breadcrumbs, He wants you to find Him. God doesn't hide things *from* you, He hides things *for* you. Proverbs 2:1-5 (NIV) describes God's intentions: *My son, if you accept my words and store up my commands within you, turning your ear to wisdom and applying your heart to understanding—indeed, if you call out for insight and cry aloud for understanding, and if you look for it as for silver and search for it as for hidden treasure, then you will understand the fear of the LORD and find the knowledge of God.*

By the end of the day, I had exhausted myself searching and obsessing over it, and finally, in my tired silence, a thought came to me: I do know a few people – in fact, five – who could write a $10,000 check as if it were like picking up a latte at a Starbucks drive-through. In five phone calls, Invisible Angels could have everything it needed by the end of the afternoon. I thought about the five people I would call and I prayed. Nothing elaborate, just a very simple, "Lord, let these be my jars."

The next morning, the first call was to my high school friend Guy, who, within the first ten seconds, enthusiastically and joyfully said, "Ted, what you guys are doing is fantastic! I can't do ten thousand dollars, but I can do five thousand dollars. I hope that will help!"

Hanging up with Guy, I thought this would all be solved in the next twenty minutes. As if God were saying, "You're getting close . . . closer . . . keep going." The next three calls produced significant promise, just not now. Just as I was about to call the fifth person, my phone rang, and it was him. It was my friend

Anthony, who was last on my list to call. He wanted to know how *Hidden Angels* was doing.

"Hey, Anthony, Invisible Angels is doing great! I was just about to call you. Our direct air-carrier certification is just around the corner, and we've hit a snag."

I explained the maintenance issue and told him we needed about $50,000 to cover our maintenance and insurance needs. I asked him for a $10,000 donation, and while he paused, I understood I might have overstepped a boundary, but I certainly thought twenty-five years of friendship was strong enough, and besides, he was the one who called me.

He offered an odd response: "Well, I am having dinner with a friend tomorrow night; let me talk to him and I'll let you know."

Anthony is a friend I have had for quite a while. We know each other well, and while he does not know Jesus, I know him well enough to know he is thinking about eternity and where he will spend it. He knows that we are destined for a *somewhere* after this life, and I know that he knows there is a God. I know he sees Christ in me because he has told me in the past, "Maybe I would get more support if I were to lay off the Christianity."

I laugh every time I hear that from him. That's a sign God is working.

The payoff in this part of the story did not come with Anthony. He had not come to Christ yet. He did not support Invisible Angels on this phone call, nor this season, but Anthony is still a riddle God has not let me solve. Sometimes God leads you in a direction that does not seem to work out, but we do not know the whole picture. We do not know what God is doing behind the scenes or even in front of the scenes, like way in front of us, like twenty miles upstream in Adam.

I kept him in this story because he was last on my list to call that day, and he called me! He called me at the exact time I was going to call him. That says God is behind this; I just cannot figure out the details. It does not matter as long as I keep moving forward, listening, remaining obedient, and praying for Anthony.

However, the payoff came after the five phone calls, with a few other donations coming in, giving us the $10,000 needed to make the next maintenance payment, right on time.

Things don't happen logically in God's kingdom. The first five chapters of Joshua are proof of an uphill battle. In Joshua 1, just as the Israelites were about to cross the Jordan into the promised land, God told them to be strong and courageous multiple times, and *"do not turn from [the law] to the right or to the left"* (verse 7) and to prepare for a season of battles. Then, after crossing the Jordan, the first thing God had them do was stop and be circumcised, leaving their entire military unable to move, probably for a month. This doesn't follow our logic, but this was how God prepared the Israelites for the season ahead, and how God received the glory.

Running uphill is God pointing us in the direction of running closer to Him. The circumcisions the Israelites faced after crossing the Jordan were a covenant, designed for the next level of spiritual proximity and greater obedience. We were originally designed for obedience, and the conflicts we face and the winds we go against are designed to push us closer to God.

The closer we come to God, the more we know who He is, and His will for our lives comes into focus by knowing who He is. God will always equip you beforehand for what He has called you into. He will never let you go into a battle ill-equipped.

There are three passages, all letters from Paul, guaranteeing this eternal truth.

- Hebrews 13:20-21 (NIV): *Now may the God of peace, who through the blood of the eternal covenant brought back from the dead our Lord Jesus, that great Shepherd of the sheep, equip you with everything good for doing his will, and may he work in us what is pleasing to him, through Jesus Christ, to whom be glory for ever and ever. Amen.*

- Romans 8:28 (NIV): *And we know that in all things God works for the good of those who love him, who have been called according to his purpose.*

- Philippians 4:13 (NIV): *I can do all this through him who gives me strength.*

These are the guarantees we have. Even though Joshua was promised the promised land, he still had to fight for it, and every battle Joshua fought was uphill.

I was in a new place in my faith. I had a front-row seat to the miracles God had been delivering for the past three years, and now God was really calling me to *get out of the boat.* I jumped out, but as soon as I took a few steps on the water, the wind and waves would pound against me, and I'd start to sink. I couldn't keep myself from looking at them.

It had become cyclical, and I was doing this repeatedly, just falling and failing headfirst into unbelief. One night, when I invited Maria, our new accounting volunteer, to dinner to get better acquainted and chat about Invisible Angels, she unleashed a deluge of biblical truth on me in a single sentence, instantly changing my perspective and keeping me on top of the waves.

I love strong personalities. We have the authority given to us by Christ, and I see many people who go about their lives unaware of their spiritual authority, failing even to recognize it, let alone use it. Maria is firmly seated in her authority. She is a strong believer, very smart, has a strong personality, and possesses a natural humility that is rare. This is the kind of person I want on the Invisible Angels' team – someone who can speak truth in love, doing it so swiftly that you barely realize what happened, or, in this case, like a tank driving right over you.

As we sat down, I started complaining about my woes, and she was having none of it. After about a minute, Maria looked at me with an exasperated look, like a mother about to scold her child, and, slightly raising her voice, she firmly said, "The longer you freak out about this, the longer it's going to take."

It felt like ten gallons of cold water were dumped right over my head. She was exactly right. We can't do anything to speed God up, but we can slow Him down. Unbelief is the fastest way to slow God down, and I was slamming on the brakes.

That night, I walked out of the restaurant asking a simple question: "How well do I know God?" Furthering the conversation with myself, I stood face-to-face with this one statement: "Look at where He has taken you and the miracles that He has done up to this point. Why on earth are you freaking out?"

God's will for your life is revealed by knowing Him, not by doing something. That includes not worrying about how He will provide. We cannot view our Christ-placed circumstances through an emotional lens of our experience. We need to realize God put us here to begin with, created the circumstances we are in, and He will provide the path through. Not over, not around, and not under, but through. This is where spiritual strength is created. We need to view God's plan through His Word and His promises. That can take time.

Just think about where God took Moses. Back in Egypt, Moses wanted to kill all the Egyptians one at a time, but in God's plan, He wiped them all out at once, just forty years later. God's will probably won't align with your righteous desires; God will do it differently. He will put *His* footprint on your circumstances, not yours.

Big miracles were happening every week at the beginning of Invisible Angels, but I had childlike faith then. God was providing, and I had little else to depend on other than Him.

So, what changed? Simply, I started to look at my situation

through a worldly lens, and not through the perspective of what God was doing. It was so much easier when I only had a vision and nothing else. Once airplanes, bank accounts, and federal agencies got involved, I started to look at them and their requirements instead of the One who provided all of that. With one comment, Maria instantly brought me back to the perspective of what God was doing.

This was like crossing the Jordan. My entire perspective flipped from insurmountable impossibilities to seeing how God was setting us up for another miracle. Over the next few weeks, all the documentation we had to submit to the FAA started coming back with an "Approval" in the email's subject line.

The documentation we had to create for Invisible Angels was staggering; even more staggering were the FAA safety officials who had to read through all of it. The biggest document was a 550-page compliance document, spelling out how Invisible Angels would comply with every CFR Part 91, 119, and 135 regulation.

We had to have our seat-back safety cards, seat-belt signs, and preflight safety briefings approved, down to the last detail of our operation; everything had to be approved by the FAA. Finally, the Excel spreadsheet with over 350 items on it, eighteen months earlier, wound down to a close. We were done.

A phone call came ten days later: "Ted, good news! We are processing your air-carrier certificate this week. You should have it in the mail next week. Congratulations! You guys are official!"

Overjoyed and relieved, Invisible Angels was now official, but one problem remained. Our airplane was still disassembled in an FAA maintenance facility, with a $25,000 bill fast approaching. At this point, we had about $600 in the bank and hadn't even considered the upcoming insurance payment. However, I stopped worrying. If God wants the plane to sit there, then it sits there. I was still praying, but it was not my problem. Invisible Angels had been prayed for by everyone on our prayer team and everyone I knew. Then, as most modern-day miracles begin, I received a phone call.

A human trafficking rescue organization we worked with over the past few years, Heritage of Hope, had entered a new season. The director, Rachel, recently had her first baby, and, after many months of prayerful consideration, decided to close the organization. Rachel and the entire team at Heritage of Hope admired Invisible Angels' work. We had conducted several rescue flights together over the past few years and shared some amazing success stories. As part of Heritage of Hope's dissolution, they wanted to make a large donation to Invisible Angels – just in time.

That same week, the maintenance facility called to tell me they were wrapping up the inspection on the airplane, and a final bill would be ready within the next few days. The insurance also needed to be paid. With the fresh witness of what God did through Heritage of Hope, I was simply watching how God would deliver.

At this point, I knew the final maintenance bill would be around $25,000, and the insurance bill would be $12,000, both due at the same time. The donation was enough to make a dent in the maintenance bill, but not to cover it completely. I knew God was preparing us for another miracle. Calling the insurance company to let them know the plane was coming out of maintenance, a question popped into my head that I had never thought of asking before: "Can we finance our insurance premium?"

"Oh yes, absolutely!"

On a phone call, with a simple question, that $12,000 bill was reduced to a completely manageable monthly payment. The problem was solved upstream, before it even became an issue.

If you have gotten this far in this story, you probably have figured out that I am not twenty-five, thirty-five, or even forty-five years old – I have retirement and brokerage accounts for the season of life I'm in. Anyway, about eighteen months earlier, my financial advisor suggested investing in a series of tech stocks. Barely knowing how to operate my iPhone, but knowing everybody who didn't have one already, wanted one, and that the right technology would only grow, I said to go ahead.

I know nothing about the stock market or investing, but my advisor was pretty conservative and had done very well so far. In the middle of all this, I just happened to pull up the account because I hadn't seen it in a while and was shocked. It had exploded over the past year. Obviously, I was thrilled, but retirement was nowhere on my radar now, and I thought about the tax bill I would be facing. I called my accountant and asked what my tax liability would be. He gave me a surprisingly large number that just happened to be the same number Invisible Angels would owe.

Second Kings 4:2 hit me. My jars! This was one of my jars! I had it! I could pay that amount to the IRS or donate that amount to Invisible Angels. One of the easiest decisions I ever made.

A week later, our aircraft was nearing completion. Final maintenance checks and test flights were being carried out, and we were expecting a final $25,000 bill. But when the email came with the final amount, it was slightly different from what was promised. I sat there, shocked again, staring in disbelief at the screen.

The maintenance company knocked $11,000 off the final bill. They had overestimated the time and materials and waited until the very end to tell us. Our financial problem was solved before it became an issue. Once again, God solved this problem proactively. Everything was covered. We had an airplane and were operational; with my donation, we even had a bit of a surplus, enough to get us through six or seven flights, probably until the end of the year.

We took delivery of our aircraft in late September 2024, and without a single announcement that Invisible Angels was operational again, we immediately started getting calls for flights. Working with Her Song – part of Tim Tebow's organization in Jacksonville, Florida – Glori, who started her own organization, Free Indeed; and One More Child in Tampa, Invisible Angels was able to get four survivors out of horrible situations during September and October. We finished the year by giving a fifth survivor a Christmas reunification with her family, whom she hadn't seen in years.

Providing those flights as Invisible Angels, the official Part 135 air carrier, was the arrival at the most glorious mountaintop I have ever experienced with God. Not only witnessing everything, but being the primary participant brought Ephesians 3:20 (NIV) to life: *Now to him who is able to do immeasurably more than all we ask or imagine, according to his power that is at work within us.*

But there was more. It brought the entire preceding paragraph to life! Ephesians 3:20 puts an exclamation point on Ephesians 3:14-19 (NIV):

> *For this reason I kneel before the Father, from whom*
> *every family in heaven and on earth derives its*
> *name. I pray that out of his glorious riches he may*
> *strengthen you with power through his Spirit in your*
> *inner being, so that Christ may dwell in your hearts*
> *through faith. And I pray that you, being rooted and*
> *established in love, may have power, together with all*
> *the Lord's holy people, to grasp how wide and long*
> *and high and deep is the love of Christ, and to know*
> *this love that surpasses knowledge—that you may be*
> *filled to the measure of all the fullness of God.*

This final paragraph in Ephesians 3 describes my entire experience from when the FAA shut us down until we flew our first flight as an official Part 135 air carrier. Along with reaching the mountaintop, this season was also one of the most difficult in my walk with Christ ever. It wasn't that I questioned Him or His provision; it was more a matter of how.

How are you going to do this? Where is this money going to come from? How are we going to get through this? I knew Jesus and I would get through it, but I could only see one way. It's in Ephesians 3:16 (NIV) that Paul says, *I pray that out of his glorious riches he may strengthen you with power through his Spirit in your inner being.*

Strengthen you with power through his Spirit in your inner being. That is what God was doing the entire time. God was strengthening my spirit by stretching my faith, isolating my options, and dissolving my expectations until the only way I could see through was the path He would provide. I saw God move financial and personal mountains and toss them into the sea. This season was all uphill, but as high as the hills were, the miracles were even higher. That is the payoff, and that is where the reward is: the witness of God providing a way through when there is no way.

Along with an operational air carrier providing rescue and recovery flights for human trafficking survivors, a bigger result emerged at the end of this season. A seismic shift occurred in my prayer life with the small change of a couple of words. Rather than asking God to provide, I started asking God to show me what this looks like to Him. *What does the solution look like in your eyes, Lord? Show me how You are going to solve this and make a way.*

The way through will never look like you think it will. It will always be different, completely outside your realm of expectations. The way through will bear His footprint, because when people see it, they will see Him, not you.

CHAPTER 13

PEOPLE

"'For I was hungry and you gave me something to eat, I was thirsty and you gave me something to drink, I was a stranger and you invited me in, I needed clothes and you clothed me, I was sick and you looked after me, I was in prison and you came to visit me.' Then the righteous will answer him, 'Lord, when did we see you hungry and feed you, or thirsty and give you something to drink? When did we see you a stranger and invite you in, or needing clothes and clothe you? When did we see you sick or in prison and go to visit you?' The King will reply, 'Truly I tell you, whatever you did for one of the least of these brothers and sisters of mine, you did for me.'" (Matthew 25:35-40 NIV)

I heard a good story a while back that describes church people to a T. It's a bit of a historical story, so indulge me for a bit.

A few weeks after Hirohito's surrender, ending World War II, an expedition team was surveying islands in the South Pacific. Researching and mapping the area as newly acquired US territories, the PBY Catalina amphibious aircraft, with a crew of three, was flying low over a chain of small islands when they noticed an open fire and several small structures on one tiny, deserted island. Circling back and descending to just fifty feet over the water to get a closer look, they noticed a male figure running out to the beach, furiously waving his hands. The PBY circled back again in a low pass, signaling to the man that he had been seen. The aircraft circled one last time and made a water landing near the beach of the tiny island. Landing in the lee, the plane turned toward the shore and beached itself as the thin male figure joyfully stood there, realizing he had finally been rescued.

As the crew exited the aircraft, they were greeted by Lieutenant John J. Simpson, a P-51 pilot who had been shot down several months earlier. Simpson was in remarkably good condition, except for seriously needing a haircut and a new set of clothes. He was in fantastic shape after surviving on a diet of fresh seafood, fruits, and vegetables.

The crew noticed three small huts Simpson had built during his eighteen months on the island. All three were exquisitely built. Gladly obliging a tour, Simpson showed the crew the first hut, his primary residence, which was quite large, well thought-out, and complete with three rooms and even a bathroom. Deeply impressed, the crew asked about the other two huts on the island.

"Well, that one's my church, and the other one is the church I used to go to."

Churches would be great places if it weren't for the people.

People are people; you take yourself with you no matter where you go. Just think of all the people who annoy you and avoid you, cheat on their taxes, talk about you behind your back, and steal your parking spaces. They all go to your church and may even be living next door to you in heaven. Before being filled with the Holy Spirit, the twelve disciples spent too much time arguing with one another over petty matters, dropping snide remarks, and being nasty. They were rendered unable to do what Jesus was trying to teach them to do, frustrating Him to no end, resulting in Matthew 17:17 (NIV): *"You unbelieving and perverse generation," Jesus replied, "how long shall I stay with you? How long shall I put up with you? Bring the boy here to me."*

The Living Bible translation reads, *"Oh, you stubborn, faithless people! How long shall I bear with you?"*

And the Amplified Bible translation says, *"You unbelieving and perverted generation, how long shall I be with you? How long shall I put up with you?"*

It is pretty clear Jesus had many "eye-rolling moments" with all twelve of them.

I want to end the Invisible Angels' story with people, because God, through people, created Invisible Angels.

My FAA colleague, Dave, was instrumental in shaping me into a professional, safety-focused Part 135 pilot. I couldn't have gotten through the check rides and oral exams without his coaching.

Bill gave me an airplane, and Brian, Craig, Robert, Kareena, and Kelly were all early donors to Invisible Angels when no one else was. There were several people in my orbit who could have written a check for the first two years, but God brought the funding in $25 at a time. That's where I saw God's blessings through God's most prized and precious creation – us, His people. The belief people have in Invisible Angels means more to me than the money, because they see God's vision and what God is doing through me, or hopefully both.

Invisible Angels is also not alone when it comes to God starting human trafficking organizations. Free Indeed, Selah Freedom, Life Recaptured, Created of Tampa, Camille Place, Missing Peace, Her Song, Heritage of Hope, and many others started the same way: a God-planted vision and then one God-miracle after another.

Laurie Swink, one of the founders of Selah Freedom, knew right away that God planted His vision in me the moment I came bouncing through her office. Having never met her before, I was introduced to her by a friend from a Bible study, and we set up a time to meet. Within the first ten seconds of walking into her office, I was going on and on about how God was starting an air-rescue organization before Invisible Angels ever had a website, business cards, or an airplane.

As we waited on the Lord, the relationships and early donors started to come, financing everything we would need in the beginning. That all came through people.

Bill, someone I had never met who lived about one thousand miles away, donated the airplane.

The 501(c)(3) approval came from an IRS office worker who most likely expedited and approved it that same day.

All the donated items, the aircraft tug, people's time, and everyone on the prayer team came through people. I have seen God's light shine brightly through people these past seven years. People will be not only your biggest asset but also your only asset. People were also the biggest challenge.

God always flips the script and transforms impossible situations – surrounded by brick walls covered with barbed wire and broken glass – into tremendous blessings, leaving you a couple of rungs higher on the ladder than before. God used the FAA inspectors who shut down Invisible Angels for a season; through that season, it became safer, more professional, and better prepared for flying passengers, as well as being the only Part 135 direct air carrier (to date) providing air rescue and recovery transport for human trafficking survivors.

The challenges and trials are also where God grew me. My discernment was stretched to new levels, along with my faith.

Quitting drinking opened up time for hours alone and undistracted, allowing me to hear the Holy Spirit and getting to know Him. In 2024, I spent a week at the School of the Prophets at Bethel Church in Redding, California, and I wouldn't have been able to hear the Holy Spirit's promptings had I not gone through those trials and challenges.

Invisible Angels has also been a tremendous witness. I feel God's presence every time I tell His story. The hearing at the FAA, all the doctors and nurses in the hospitals, all the people I work with, and everyone I still come into contact with hear the story of how God started the Invisible Angels' ministry. Whether they wanted to hear the story or not, all left amazed. God told me to tell His story, and I still do. I have no idea what He will do with it, but I am sure it will be glorious.

It is also people whom God uses who will encourage you or even laugh at you. After God told me that my next season would be in aviation ministry, having been a pilot for about fifteen minutes, people in my church at the time laughed at me. They called me a dreamer, snickered at me, and thought I was crazy. Well, I am. That's probably the biggest reason God chose me. I was mad, and perhaps it was justified, but after a few days of prayer, I realized I didn't get mad at them for laughing at me; I got angry at them for not seeing God's vision.

A few weeks after I had left the church, I had dinner with one of the leaders, just to make sure we could still sit down, break bread, and be Christian brothers. It dawned on me during our dinner: he had probably never heard God like that before, and most likely didn't think it was possible.

The best advice I can give if you have been called into ministry or decide to start one is: as long as your ministry aligns with God's will, He will bless you and make a way. Read John 14, the entire chapter, every day for about a month. Memorize it. Then confirm it is God's will through significant – and I do mean significant – time in prayer and confirmation through the Word and through people.

If your call to start a ministry is directly from God, and you know it is from God, and there is indisputable evidence that it is from God, then expect trouble, and expect trouble from people. People will laugh at you and call you crazy. Don't listen and don't get mad. Look at their response from their perspective. They probably come from a place on the emotional spectrum anywhere from fear to jealousy. Be kind and put some distance between you and them.

The Enemy will come at you full force and do everything and anything, from chemo wards to courtrooms, to try and stop you, and that will all be through people. Put a prayer team around you and meet regularly; start putting solid, prayerful believers who believe God can do the impossible, in your orbit.

Remember, two or three believers can change the course of history, and don't ever forget that. That could, and should, be you. And after you get started, don't get discouraged. So many people came forward and volunteered to help, and I never saw them again. That's human nature, too. It is through people that you will see God move. Get to know people well before partnering with them. Spend time with them; go away for a weekend or on a road trip to learn their true motivations.

Several people joined Invisible Angels, and after a year or so of getting to know them, I discovered their hearts were not in the right place. Go at God's speed, and remember that this will not work on your time frame or your strategic plan. Whenever you face circumstances that don't make sense, you will see God make a way. Just remember, He has been there the entire time.

God created Invisible Angels for the trafficking survivors. There are no words to describe the horror that these innocent individuals have gone through and are currently going through. This

Auschwitz-level trauma is happening to children as young as two years old, and to women and men in their late forties and older.

The horror stories I have heard range from mothers pouring acid on their children's bodies because they snitched their parents out to the police, to being thrown into a retaining pond and executed in the middle of the night. The stories get worse and worse. Over 60 percent of trafficking victims are trafficked by their parents or family members.

Social service caseworkers are trafficking children in the foster care system because they are an easy target, and no one will believe them if they are reported. Some traffickers have hammered nails into their victims' feet so they won't run, and fathers have kidnapped their own children to put them into a child pornography ring and profit from the product produced. There have been several times at conferences while hearing the testimony of law enforcement and others concerning situations so horribly extreme that I have had to leave the room.

God sees all of this, and rest assured, His wrath is coming. Isaiah 3:11 (NIV) says, *Woe to the wicked! Disaster is upon them! They will be paid back for what their hands have done.* The traffickers and others who have done this to God's precious ones will surely stand before Him one day. We have that assurance.

It is still difficult to have peace when I hear these stories. Proverbs 16:4 (NIV) says, *The LORD works out everything to its proper end—even the wicked for a day of disaster.* This plays through my mind when I hear the background situations and circumstances of the survivors we have taken to safety.

God's Word is the only thing that anyone can hold on to when surrounded by these horrific stories. I can't tell you why God chose me for this, probably because I am the least likely, but hopefully, I have explained beyond the shadow of a doubt that this is God's will and God is clearly in this fight. And He always wins.

GOD IS STILL IN THE MIRACLE BUSINESS

Scattered throughout the country is an intricate network of safe houses and residential rescue facilities for human trafficking survivors. Most, if not all, of these facilities are Christ-centered and Christian-founded, meaning that nearly every one of them was initiated by God planting a vision in the founder's soul, mind, and spirit, and the miracles began to unfold from there. *God Is in This Fight* tells yet another miracle story in God's fight against the horrors of human trafficking – a fight which, as promised, belongs to God, as stated in Exodus 14:13-14.

Many people have the same question: *How can I help?* You can make a significant impact by partnering with dedicated support and rescue organizations through small monthly donations. To illustrate, if one thousand people each contribute just $10 a month, that amounts to $10,000 monthly, which goes a long way in supporting their vital work. Consider partnering with safe homes such as Selah Freedom (www.selahfreedom.org), Life Recaptured (www.liferecaptured.org), Created of Tampa (www. createdwomen.com), Camille Place (www.camilleplace.com), Missing Peace (www.missingpeaceministry.org), and Her Song (www.hersong.org), as well as placement organizations like Free Indeed (www.iamfreeindeed.com). Support organizations such as Invisible Angels (www.invisibleangels.org) and The Freedom Aviation Network (www.freedomaviationnetwork.org). These are all run by highly trained professional staff and volunteers.

Beyond financial support, two key items top the list of what these organizations need: funding and awareness. Have conversations about human trafficking within your community, from youth groups to corporate gatherings. You can contact any human trafficking organization, and they would be more than happy to provide a speaker for an event to raise awareness and educate others. In fact, hearing a speaker from Maranatha Freedom on this issue inspired the creation of Invisible Angels, which eventually led me to use an airplane to transport trafficking survivors to safety, opening a new season and ministry in my life.

Every Christian should have this same question: *What is God's will for my life?* That question can only be answered by getting closer to Him, outlined so clearly in Jeremiah 29:12-13 (NIV): *"Then you will call on me and come and pray to me, and I will listen to you. You will seek me and find me when you seek me with all your heart."*

God is still in the miracle business. Every organization listed above has the same story: an idea planted by God, cultivated by obedience and time, and God birthed another organization in this fight. The same can be true for you. You can also be part of this fight. It begins with prayer, followed by reaching out to these organizations. As you start with fundraising and raising awareness, you will see where God will take you.

Ted Greenfield, M.Ed.

ABOUT THE AUTHOR

Ted Greenfield, M.Ed. is the founder and director of Invisible Angels, a nonprofit organization providing air transportation for survivors of human trafficking. A commercially rated pilot, Ted retired from the Federal Aviation Administration (FAA) in the spring of 2025, where he served as a multimedia producer, creating safety messaging and training for air traffic controllers and pilots. Before his time at the FAA, Ted served as a senior instructional systems designer contractor at Lockheed Martin and was the executive producer and internet managing editor for Voice of America's Learning English.

Ted made plans, but his steps were directed by God (Proverbs 16:9), resulting in a diverse background – from special education teacher, to improv comedian, to television producer. Ted then navigated the evolving internet landscape of the late 1990s while owning a small online training and multimedia development company until 2008, after which he worked for the FAA until 2025.